Trevor Lynch's White Nationalist Guide to the Movies

by

Trevor Lynch

Edited by Greg Johnson

Foreword by Kevin MacDonald

Counter-Currents Publishing Ltd.
San Francisco
2012

Copyright © 2012 by Greg Johnson
All rights reserved

Cover design by
Kevin I. Slaughter

Published in the United States by
COUNTER-CURRENTS PUBLISHING LTD.
P.O. Box 22638
San Francisco, CA 94122
USA
http://www.counter-currents.com/

Hardcover ISBN: 978-1-935965-43-5
Paperback ISBN: 978-1-935965-44-2
E-book ISBN: 978-1-935965-45-9

Library of Congress Cataloging-in-Publication Data

Lynch, Trevor, 1971-
Trevor Lynch's white nationalist guide to the movies / by Trevor Lynch ; edited by Greg Johnson ; foreword by Kevin B. MacDonald.
p. cm.
Summary: "Collection of film reviews written from a White Nationalist perspective, highlighting the presence of anti-White propaganda and an identifiable Jewish agenda, as well as positive pro-White messages, in 32 different films."-- Provided by publisher.
ISBN 978-1-935965-43-5 (hardcover : alk. paper) -- ISBN 978-1-935965-44-2 (pbk. : alk. paper) -- ISBN 978-1-935965-45-9 (ebook)
1. Motion pictures--Reviews. I. Johnson, Greg, 1971- II. Title.
III. Title: White nationalist guide to the movies.
PN1995.L96 2012
791.43'75--dc23
2012011689

Contents

Foreword by Kevin MacDonald ♦ iii

Editor's Note by Greg Johnson ♦ vii

1. Introduction: Why I Write ♦ 1

The Lord of the Rings
2. *The Fellowship of the Ring* ♦ 7
3. *The Two Towers* ♦ 11
4. *The Return of the King* ♦ 18
5. "The Scouring of the Shire" ♦ 22

Christopher Nolan
6. *Batman Begins* ♦ 27
7. *The Dark Knight* ♦ 31
8. *The Dark Knight Rises* ♦ 42
9. *Inception* ♦ 54

Guillermo del Toro
10. *Cronos, The Devil's Backbone, & Pan's Labyrinth* ♦ 57
11. *Hellboy* ♦ 63
12. *Hellboy II: The Golden Army* ♦ 68

Quentin Tarantino
13. *Pulp Fiction* ♦ 73
14. *Kill Bill: Vol. I* ♦ 97
15. *Inglourious Basterds* ♦ 102
16. *Django Unchained* ♦ 109

The *Matrix* Movies
17. *The Matrix Reloaded* ♦ 115
18. *The Matrix Revolutions* ♦ 121

The Twilight Saga
19. *Twilight* ♦ 126
20. *New Moon* ♦ 131
21. *Eclipse* ♦ 134
22. *Breaking Dawn, Part 1* ♦ 138
23. *Breaking Dawn, Part 2* ♦ 143

The Millennium Trilogy
24. *The Girl with the Dragon Tattoo* ♦ 145
25. *The Girl with the Dragon Tattoo* Remake ♦ 149
26. *The Girl Who Played with Fire* ♦ 152
27. *The Girl Who Kicked the Hornet's Nest* ♦ 156

Violence & Redemption
28. *300* ♦ 159
29. *Gangs of New York* ♦ 163
30. *A History of Violence* ♦ 168
31. *Mishima: A Life in Four Chapters* ♦ 173
32. *The Baader-Meinhof Complex* ♦ 185

About the Author ♦ 190

Foreword

Trevor Lynch provides us with a highly literate, insightful, and even philosophical perspective on film — one that will send you running to the video rental store for a look at some very worthwhile movies — although he is also quite willing to tell you what not to see, e.g.: "No white person should pay a nickel to see [*The Girl with the Dragon Tattoo*]." He sees movies without the usual blinders. He is quite aware that because Hollywood is controlled by Jews, one must typically analyze movies for their propaganda value in the project of white dispossession.

His review of *The Matrix Reloaded* is a great example of calling attention to the anti-white animus that pervades Hollywood now: "Looking at a movie like this, you would almost believe that White civilization could not have been created without the contributions of blacks, browns, yellows, Jews," etc.

Naturally, in such an environment, one must expect that supervillains will be Nazis or obvious Aryans, or at least they won't look Jewish or have Jewish names. On the other hand, "superheroes tend to function as symbolic proxies for Jews" — fighting for the values of egalitarian, anti-racialist universalism that have come to define the values of the Jewish Diaspora in the West (but are anathema to Jews in Israel).

However, from my reading of this collection of essays, Stieg Larsson's *Millennium Trilogy* movies would seem to be pretty much the worst sort of media imaginable, creating an upside-down world of a contemporary Sweden filled with native Swedish rapists and highly placed Nazis. Larsson has completely internalized a Jewish mindset to the point that in his fiction Jewish lives are more important than non-Jewish lives. "In Guillaume Faye's terms, [people like Larsson] are textbook ethnomasochists and xenophiles. They would prefer their own people to be murdered rather than Jews (Jews above all) and assorted totemic 'others.' Sick, sick people."

The fact that writers like Larsson have a wide following and are able to have their work made into popular movies is a telling testimony to our time.

However, despite Hollywood's pervasive hatred of whites and our culture, a precious few movies do speak to our ideals and hopes for a return to an explicit sense of white consciousness and destiny. *The Lord of the Rings* trilogy is certainly in this category because of its message—so resonant today—of saving the people and culture of the West from dark hordes led by evil schemers with names like Sauron that sound alien to the European spirit and, to my ears at least, even have Semitic overtones.

Lynch also notes that many other movies have powerful messages that are dangerous to the *status quo*, but they appear *"only in the mouths of monsters"*—such as the Joker in Christopher Nolan's *The Dark Knight*. The Joker is a Nietzschean *Übermensch*: unafraid of death, he cares nothing for money, and he has no respect for society's rules—indeed, no moral compunctions at all. Such a monster is dangerous to the contemporary Western *Zeitgeist* which depends most of all on a strong sense of moral universalism and the value of all life, even when it means the suicide of the West. Moral principles trump even survival as a culture and a people. Such a moral universalism is antithetical to the particularist imperative of white survival.

Unfortunately, the Joker cares nothing for his people and culture: he is the epitome of radical and even pathological individualism. But a cadre of people who are committed to Western survival, who are unafraid of death, uninterested in the easily available decadent pleasures of the contemporary world, and without the moral scruples of egalitarian universalism would be dangerous indeed to the current *Zeitgeist*. Of course, this would require a sense of moral commitment to the culture and people of the West—including the many whites who have been corrupted or are wanting in other ways—that is quite foreign to the Joker.

But the best example of wisdom from the mouths of monsters is Bill the Butcher from Martin Scorsese's *Gangs of New York*, who states what is unthinkable in today's America, committed as it is to White displacement—that "America is an organic community, a community of blood: a community purchased by the blood of its founders to safeguard the blood of their posterity.... [Bill the Butcher] sees that Lincoln's artificial 'Union' devoted to the 'proposition' of equality is the mortal enemy of an organic community based on blood." I imagine that more than a few whites in the audience agreed with those sentiments.

Lynch shows that even the most popular fare may have implicit messages that conflict with the general anti-white narrative of Hollywood, if only because Hollywood sees these films as a way of making money. For example, the first *Twilight* movie paints a picture of an implicitly white world that accentuates the beauty of white people. And I was surprised to find that there are still vestiges of popular culture that celebrate traditional sexual values: "*The Twilight Saga* is an *explicit* defense of virginity followed by marriage and motherhood and an *explicit* rejection of pre-marital sex and sexual promiscuity." And there is the message that "manliness is a good thing: women are attracted to primal strength and aggression."

Another example is *A History of Violence*, which upholds the value of masculine men who are willing to form families but also willing and able to fight for the protection of the family and for civilization itself—an image that is all too rare in an age where gangsta rap stars are far more likely to be promoted by Hollywood as appropriate role models for young males.

There is much else here—philosophical thoughts on hedonism, post-modernism, decadence, aesthetics, honor and pride versus self-preservation and money, cultural integrity versus multiculturalism—all framed within a pro-white worldview. Trevor Lynch's collection is a must read for anyone attempting to understand the deep undercurrents of the contemporary culture of the West.

Kevin MacDonald
Long Beach
November 28, 2012

Editor's Note

I wrote my first movie review in the fall of 2001. The movie was David Lynch's *Mulholland Drive*. The publication was *Vanguard News Network*, then my favorite White Nationalist site. I was inspired to write specifically White Nationalist movie reviews by VNN's Mark Rivers. Later I discovered the movie reviews of John "Yggdrasil" Gardner, which set a whole new standard of sophistication and insight.

Initially, I wrote under the pen name "The Cat Lady," because I was annoyed at the calls for White Nationalists to soften our message to attract more women. So the idea of a female author who was more extreme than VNN editor Alex Linder struck me as funny. I named this persona "The Cat Lady" as a tribute to Savitri Devi, who remains a major inspiration to my work.

Sure "The Cat Lady" is a dumb pen name. But the internet is full of such monikers, and I am sure they all seemed clever at the time. I regretted it almost immediately, though, because I put a lot of work into my reviews, and I thought that nobody would recommend a review by "The Cat Lady."

But when my second review, which dealt with Peter Jackson's *The Fellowship of the Ring*, appeared in December of 2001, it went viral in spite of the pen name. I am told that it was actually quoted in an article in *The Washington Times* and also read aloud and discussed on an Atlanta-area talk radio show. (I have never learned the name of the show.)

Eventually, I changed the pen name to T. C. Lynch (the racist formerly known as "The Cat Lady"). Then, with a few keystrokes, I reassigned T. C. Lynch's "gender," dubbing him Trevor Caden Lynch, then just Trevor Lynch.

The rationale of the new pen name is simple. First, it had to have the same initial letters as The Cat Lady. Beyond that, David Lynch is my favorite director, and Trevor is the name of a friend and fellow film buff.

All internet silliness aside, I am very proud of these reviews and essays. I also think they make a positive contribution to White Nationalism, for reasons outlined below in the Introduction. Thus I think they are worthy of being republished in book form. I have made many minor corrections, but I have not attempted to eliminate repetitions in the reviews of such series as *The Lord of the Rings*, *The Twilight Saga*, *The Millennium Trilogy*, etc.

And now for my Oscar speech: I wish to thank Alex Linder, editor of *Vanguard News Network*, and Kevin MacDonald, editor of *The Occidental Observer*, for first publishing some of these pieces. The rest appeared under my own editorship, first at *TOQ Online* then at Counter-Currents/*North American New Right*.

I owe special thanks to Kevin MacDonald for his splendid Foreword and to Edmund Connelly, F. Roger Devlin, Jack Donovan, and James J. O'Meara for their blurbs. I also wish to thank Collin Cleary, Michael Polignano, Gregory Hood, the original Trevor, Matt Parrott, Matthew Peters, Raven Gatto, Kevin Slaughter, and many others who cannot be named for all their contributions, tangible and intangible, to this book.

Finally, if I may allow myself one last Cat Lady moment, I want to thank all you wonderful people out there in the dark.

Greg Johnson
San Francisco
March 7, 2012

WHY I WRITE

Why do I write movie and television reviews from a White Nationalist perspective? It's complicated.

First and foremost, I write because I love film. I think that film is the realization of Richard Wagner's idea of the "complete work of art" (*Gesamtkunstwerk*), a form of art that incorporates all other art forms: music, dance, acting, sculpture, painting, architecture, etc. Film better realizes Wagner's ambitions than opera, since film can *show* things that opera merely *tells*.

By integrating so many art forms, film can communicate more, and more deeply, to more people, than any single art form. (The same is true of television; the screen is just smaller.) I loved film long before I became a White Nationalist, and I had been intending to write a book on David Lynch before I had my political awakening.

Second, I write because movies are a force. They are the greatest tool ever invented for shaping people's ideas and imaginations. In the right hands, they can be a force for good. In the wrong hands, they are a force for evil. Unfortunately, the film industry in the United States and Europe is overwhelmingly controlled by an alien and hostile people, the Jews.

Jews use movies as a tool to promote ideas and values that are destructive of my race and civilization: race-mixing and multiculturalism, white guilt and self-hatred, feminism and emasculation, the valorization of Jews and non-whites, etc. Film reviews are one way that I can fight back.

But I am often asked, "If the movies are full of anti-white propaganda, why not just boycott them altogether—and encourage others to do so as well? If you believe that Jews are using movies and television as tools of genocide against our race, then it is wrong to watch them, encourage others to watch them, or give the people behind them a single dime." I reject this argument for three reasons.

1. A complete boycott of movies and TV would be a quixotic and futile gesture. Boycotts only work if there are numerous

participants who can monitor each other to enforce compliance. If I boycotted movies and TV, I would be the only one. Nobody would join me, and if anyone did join, they would cheat. They would enjoy warm feelings of righteousness for a few minutes, then reach for the remote.

2. Moreover, movies and television are so much a part of people's lives that any White Nationalist who seriously attempted to boycott them would end up even more socially isolated and alienated than is normal for our people. Socializing with friends and family often involves watching TV and movies, or at least discussing them.

There's also a larger point here: We cannot change the world by disengaging from it. We need to engage it and turn it in our direction. If we want to make a difference, we cannot retreat from the world to preserve our purity. We need to find a way of being in the world, but not of it.

3. Boycotting TV and movies is throwing away a golden opportunity to reach our people. The film, television, and advertising industries comprise a vast number of highly intelligent, creative individuals with many billions of dollars of capital at their disposal, with which they create a 24/7 matrix of genocidal anti-white propaganda. White Nationalists cannot compete with that. Sure, we can dream of having our own mass media someday. But that will be after the revolution, not before. So what do we do in the meantime?

We can't get our people to turn off the propaganda. We can't create anywhere enough of our own television and movie propaganda to counter the establishment's. But we can teach our people to *see through* the propaganda. And all it takes is a few perceptive and talented writers, the cost of Netflix and a few movie tickets, and a few dollars a month to host a website. Yet for that small investment, we can negate the propaganda churned out by legions of enemies with billions in capital. This is asymmetrical cultural warfare at its best. Our power is limited only by our readership. But on the web, that can grow very quickly.

Furthermore, I don't just talk about specific movies and TV shows. I also illustrate the general principles of anti-white propaganda, teaching my readers how to decode propaganda in general. This has two profound effects.

1. Whenever a brainwashed person is exposed to propaganda, it reinforces the establishment message. However, when we teach people to see through propaganda, then each new exposure reinforces *our message* instead. Imagine a young man who stumbles across one of my reviews because he is reading up on a movie he wants to see. He might like my interpretation or hate it. He might even reject my claims about the propaganda content of the film. But if he is bright, he will carry away a template for viewing other films, and he will begin to see the same patterns again and again. Gradually, the establishment's power over his mind will fade, and the nagging little voice of Trevor Lynch will get louder and louder.

2. When people learn to see through anti-white propaganda, they are often shocked by its omnipresence. It is one thing to see propaganda here and there. It is another thing to see it everywhere. Even I am still shocked when I visit friends who have cable. The anti-white message is everywhere: in every cooking, cute animal, and house makeover program. You can't escape it, and that's no accident. When you see the omnipresence of the lie, you have a concrete experience of the system's totalitarian nature and genocidal intent.

There is, however, a sense in which I boycott television, and I recommend others do so as well. I don't watch broadcast television, and I refuse to pay for cable. So I don't watch commercials, and the only TV series I see are downloaded or on DVD. I don't like being "programmed." My slogan is "Program yourself." And I just don't want to spend the money.

It astonishes me how much money White Nationalists pay to people who hate them in order to have toxic propaganda piped into their homes. It is even more shocking when you compare your monthly cable bill to your monthly donations to Counter-Currents or other pro-white websites, where people are actually fighting against the lies. So if you feel the need to boycott someone, cancel your cable and subscribe to a monthly donation to Counter-Currents instead. (Just go to http://www.counter-currents.com/donate/.) Don't be the sort of person who pays to be poisoned but counts on the antidote to be free.

I don't write reviews just because I want to pan bad movies. I also want to praise good ones. And from a White Nationalist point of view, there are a lot of good movies out there.

The best movies are what I call the Goebbels Awards laureates. These are movies made by mainstream modern directors that Joseph Goebbels would not change a frame of. These include *The Lord of the Rings* trilogy, *Gangs of New York, A History of Violence, Miller's Crossing, Cabaret,* and *Quiz Show.*

Of course, most good movies that are useful from a White Nationalist perspective are also flawed, some of them slightly (like *Fight Club* or *The Dark Knight*), some of them deeply (like *Pulp Fiction* and *The Matrix*). It often takes some adroit thinking to separate the good elements from the bad.

But the potential rewards are immense. Many White Nationalists justifiably lament the decline of education and rampant cultural illiteracy. People used to learn Latin, but now they devote their brain power to memorizing sports statistics. People used to read Plato and Shakespeare, but now they stare at shining screens. Kids today know more about Batman than George Washington, more about the Battle of Helm's Deep than the Battle of Lepanto, more about Middle Earth than the Middle Ages. How can reactionary old cranks live in the past if nobody knows anything about it?

Now, I would like nothing better than to write essays about Plato, Nietzsche, and Evola for the rest of my life. And I would be doing just that, if my race were not being marched into oblivion. I want to fight, and that means I need to communicate. So I stopped lamenting other people's cultural illiteracy and started correcting my own: my pop-cultural illiteracy. Because there is no more powerful medium than film at implanting images in people's minds, and if we know those images, we can use them to communicate our ideas. And as I have shown, one can use *Pulp Fiction* to teach Plato, *Batman Begins* and *The Dark Knight* to teach Evola, Nietzsche, and Heidegger, etc.

As a writer, editor, businessman, and community organizer, I have to divide my time finely and spread myself pretty thin. But if I could delegate some of my jobs to others so I could focus full time on just one thing, I would write movie reviews. Not because it would be the most personally fulfilling, but because there is nothing I can do for our cause that is more effective at unplugging our people from the Matrix and showing them the path toward the White Republic.

Counter-Currents/North American New Right,
August 1, 2011

The Fellowship of the Ring

At one minute past midnight on Wednesday, December 19th, 2001, I was one of hundreds of people assembled in several sold-out theaters to see the Atlanta opening of *The Fellowship of the Ring*. I was astonished that hundreds of people had gathered to watch a three-hour movie starting after midnight. Surely most of these people had to be at their jobs the next morning! But, judging from their reactions as they streamed out, none of them were disappointed.

The audience was overwhelmingly white and young. The sexes were equally represented. I was impressed with how many attractive, healthy, confident people were there. Some Tolkien fanatics were dressed in costumes. There was a real feeling of community and a lot of good-natured chatter. Apparent strangers struck up conversations about the books and their expectations for the film.

But when the movie started, the whole audience sat in rapt silence. There was no fidgeting, no whispering, and not a lot of crinkling and crunching. There were some tears and sniffles later, but they were no distraction, as I was crying too. I have never experienced such a civilized and attentive audience. This is a tribute to the film. *The Fellowship of the Ring* is one of the finest movies I have ever seen. I urge every White Nationalist to see it.

I need not comment on the details of the plot. Suffice it to say that it illustrates the most serious of all themes: the fight of good against evil—in the world and in the individual soul. It has been years since I read the novels, but the film told the story as far as I remember it. One purist complained about some departures from writ. But by the end he was sold nonetheless. Still, I pitied him, because, in my ignorance and forgetfulness, I was capable of enjoying the movie without reservation. (My attachment to writ prevented me from appreciating the greatness of David Lynch's version of *Dune* until years after its release.)

I found myself moved to tears in many places. Not just because of sad events in the story, but because this movie is such a magnificent epitome of the greatness of our race and civilization that it underscores all that we have lost. The novels epitomize our Nordic myths. The Gothic and Celtic and Nordic sets and costumes epitomize Northern European architecture and decorative arts. The actors epitomize the beauties of the different varieties of our race, from the elegantly Nordic (but slightly androgynous) Elves played by Cate Blanchett, Liv Tyler, Hugo Weaving, and Orlando Bloom—to the spare, wizened Wizards played by Ian McKellen and Christopher Lee—to the magnificently brave and virile Humans played by Viggo Mortensen and Sean Bean—to the more squat and four-square types, the Dwarves (played by John Rhys-Davies) and the Hobbits (played by Elijah Wood, Ian Holm, Sean Astin, Billy Boyd, and Dominic Monaghan). I can't recall a movie with more pairs of luminous blue-eyes (Elijah Wood's and Cate Blanchett's in particular). The movie itself, so magnificently directed by Peter Jackson, gives you a glimpse of what our cinema could have been like were it not controlled by an alien and hostile race. One cannot, of course, avoid involving these parasites in the production of a film, but the content of *The Fellowship of the Ring* is entirely devoid of their corrupting ideas and influence.

Another outstanding feature of this film are the magnificent landscapes of New Zealand. No wonder the English coveted this land so much. They arrived at the other end of the Earth to find a land that encompasses all the different climates and landscapes of Northern Europe and the British Isles.

I suspect that the destroyers of our race and civilization will sell this movie as a multiculturalist, multiracialist fable—a parable of how the different races of the Fellowship can work together for a common goal. There is even a hint of miscegenation. But I do not think that this is a proper interpretation.

Here is my hypothesis. The different races of Tolkien's Fellowship, like those of Wagner's *Ring* and the myths on which both Tolkien and Wagner draw, represent different aspects of the human soul. The Elves and Wizards appear to correspond to aspects of the higher cognitive faculties of the soul. The

Elves are intuitive, wise, and self-conscious. The Wizards do not embody wisdom, but technical-instrumental rationality that can be used either for good or ill, wisdom or folly. The Humans correspond to the spirited, warlike, competitive, and honorable part of the soul. The Dwarves correspond to the appetitive part of the soul, the producer-consumer. (The Dwarves are initially dismissed as allies in the quest because they are materialistic and self-centered rather than idealistic and concerned with higher goods.) The Hobbits appear to correspond to childlike innocence and naïveté, which opens them to the wisdom of nature, characteristics they share with Siegfried.

The dynamics of the Ring Fellowship are thus an allegory for the dynamics of the soul. The great moral and existential question of Tolkien and Wagner — and of Plato and ultimately the whole Indo-European mythological tradition — is: What is the proper ordering of the soul, the proper fellowship of its parts?

If the races of the Fellowship represent different aspects of the European racial soul, what are we to make of the other races in the story? The chief villain is the Dark Lord Sauron, a devil — perhaps the Devil — who seeks to rule the world with the Ring of Power, a golden band forged in the furnaces of Mount Doom. As in Wagner, the Ring represents technology, the primal forces of nature transformed into a tool of human power, enslaving the higher aspects of the human soul (reason, honor) to the lower (greed, fear). The Dark Lord's empire is capitalism. The quest of the Fellowship is to destroy the Ring, to return its power to nature, to liberate the higher faculties of the soul from the thrall of the lower, to liberate nature from technological mastery, to annihilate capitalism.

The servants of the Dark Lord are the wizard Saruman, the nine Ringwraiths (former kings of men), the Orcs, and the Uruk-hai. Saruman and the Ringwraiths are traitorous members of the races of the Fellowship. But who are the Orcs, the hideous, greedy, treacherous, squat, squabbling servants of the Dark Lord, who feast like maggots on the corpse of murdered nature, who swarm like cockroaches through the bowels of the Earth? They are Tolkien's equivalent of Wagner's Nibelungen, who are an allegorical representation of the Jews. And then there are the Uruk-hai—the tall, muscular, aggressive, stupid, black-skinned soldiers of the Dark Lord—spawned and gestated in mud, and unleashed by Sauron and the Orcs to enslave and exterminate the fair races of the Fellowship.

As my companion and I drove away into the sprawling urban hell of Atlanta, I wondered aloud: "How can people watch a movie like that and then return to this without feeling profoundly alienated? How can they see such magnificent natural landscapes and such beautiful, organic buildings—and then feel at home in this tacky, plastic cityscape? How can they see such serious, noble, idealistic people—and then watch *Friends* and *Will and Grace*? How can they see such magnificent specimens of the white race—and then contentedly rub elbows with Negroes, Mestizos, and Jews?"

If more people took Tolkien's world to heart, this world would be finished.

Thus it is a veritable miracle that this movie was made in today's culture. The Orcs will surely recognize the threat it poses. But there is nothing they can do now to prevent the rest of the trilogy from being made and released, for Peter Jackson made all three films at the same time!

See this movie for a glimpse, here and now, of the kind of white culture we are working to create in the future.

VNN, December 20, 2001

The Two Towers

It was one minute past midnight again, exactly 364 days after the opening of *The Fellowship of the Ring*, the first of *The Lord of the Rings* movies, and I was back for the opening of *The Two Towers*. I loved the first movie so much that I was fully expecting to be disappointed. There's nowhere to go from here but down, I thought. So I was moved to tears of absolute delight that *The Two Towers* is even better than *The Fellowship of the Ring*.

The Two Towers has everything that I liked about *Fellowship*. It is powerful, poetic, and profoundly moving. It is one of the greatest movies I have ever seen. I completely share the sentiments of the friend with whom I saw it: "I wish I could live in that world. It may be grubby and dangerous, but it is more beautiful, and life is more significant."

The Lord of the Rings series is the most brilliant screen adaptation of a novel that I have ever seen. It is not always faithful to the letter of Tolkien—straying in ways that are not required by screen adaptation—but it is definitely faithful to his spirit.

It makes no concessions to political correctness and multiracialism. It contains not a shred of Jewish propaganda. This is particularly astonishing since the whole story is about different races joining together in a common quest. But Tolkien has a deeply racialist vision, and he makes it very clear that the races of the fellowship all have white features. Thus the *Rings* movies contain one of the whitest casts you will ever see. This is particularly true of *The Two Towers*, in which the people of Rohan are a beautiful collection of Nordics. As for the enemy races—the Orcs, the Uruk-hai, the Southrons, the Easterlings—they all have non-White features. Indeed, in Jackson's adaptation, the stupid, muscular, aggressive, black-skinned Uruk-hai have long, stringy, matted hair that resembles dreadlocks and they are literally born from mud.

Myth is a mirror in which we can see our souls, and as I mentioned in my review of *Fellowship*, I would argue that the different races of the fellowship actually represent different aspects of the white racial soul, and the question that animates Tolkien's story is the same that animates Wagner's *Ring*, Homer's epics, Plato's *Republic*, and much of Indo-European mythology: What is the proper internal ordering of the soul, the proper fellowship of its parts? Should we be ruled by our reason, our pride, or our desires? Is it better to be simple than cunning? Can our scientific and technological abilities to understand and master nature be ruled by wisdom and put to right use? Or are we too weak to use them without being corrupted by them, so the wisest use is not to use them at all?

Let me count the ways I liked *The Two Towers* even more than *Fellowship*.

First, the realization of the character Gollum—portrayed by Andy Serkis and a staff of computer animators—was absolutely stunning both technically and artistically. Jackson and Serkis brilliantly track the twists and turns of Gollum's tortured inner labyrinth, making the complexities of the character fully intelligible. I felt deeply for Gollum, for the shreds of decency in his soul that were overcoming the darkness until Frodo's tragic betrayal.

Second, the character of Aragorn, played beautifully by Viggo Mortensen, emerges as a genuine epic hero. In *Fellowship* Mortensen played him in such a soft-spoken and detached manner that I wondered if he could ultimately bring off the role. Now I have no doubts. In *The Two Towers*, we see Aragorn transformed from a loner to a leader of men. His teacher is King Théoden of Rohan, brilliantly played by Bernard Hill.

When Aragorn first meets Théoden, he gives the King bad counsel. He asks Théoden to spare the life of the traitor Gríma Wormtongue. Théoden does so, with disastrous consequences. Aragorn and Gandalf also urge Théoden to ride out to meet the forces of Isengard in open battle, but Théoden elects to lead his people to the fortress of Helm's Deep. When we see the armies of Isengard approach, we see the wisdom of Théoden's decision. The Rohirrim would have been slaughtered if they had joined open battle, and Helm's Deep would have held if Wormtongue had been dispatched.

But the most important lesson Théoden imparts is when

Aragorn besieges the King with pessimism about the possibility of victory. "What would you have me do?" Théoden asks, "Look at my men. Their courage hangs by a thread. If this is to be our end, then I would have them make such an end as to be worthy of remembrance." Théoden's point is that true leadership is not about calculating the chances of a favorable outcome, but about inspiring men to do noble deeds no matter what the consequences. We see Aragorn pondering this lesson and taking it to heart. First, he instills courage in a terrified young man. Then, when the King's own courage hangs by a thread, Aragorn encourages him to mount his charger and seek that end "worthy of remembrance."

Third, perhaps the greatest test of Jackson's skill in this film was the realization of Tolkien's most unlikely characters, Treebeard and his folk the Ents. I confess, I could never envision these walking, talking trees and their assault on Isengard without laughing, and I always thought them the weakest link in the novel. But Jackson made them totally believable. Treebeard is genuinely funny, but not the least bit ridiculous.

Fourth, there are a number of other new characters, all of them beautifully portrayed: Brad Dourif, my favorite movie weirdo, plays Gríma Wormtongue; Miranda Otto plays Éowyn, King Théoden's niece, and Karl Urban plays Éomer, his nephew; David Wenham plays Faramir of Gondor, the brother of Boromir.

Some favorite lines: King Théoden asks, "How did it come to this?" as his Nordic remnant prepares for the onslaught of the mud hordes, passing out arms to teenage boys and old men. It brought to mind the *Hitlerjugend* and *Volkssturm* at the end of World War II. I wonder when our "leaders" will ask the same question, and will it be too late?

The beautiful Éowyn declares that what she fears more than death or pain is "a cage," a cage that she will grow used to over time. That, of course, is the attitude of a free man or woman. Unfortunately, the majority of Whites today fear pain and death — nay, mere social disapproval — far more than chains. Thus they are slaves in spirit, if not by law. Those who prefer comfort and security to freedom have none of them in the end. Of course the majority of whites were probably like this in all times. But most of the time, the destiny of the race was determined not by the majority, but by the noble few.

Fifth, as far as I can see, the only probable Jew who played a creative role in the *Rings* movies so far is composer Howard Shore, and he is the weakest link. Shore's best work is for modern, urban, decadent, extremely Jewish movies like *Crash* and *Naked Lunch*. (His *Crash* score really is superb.) I was skeptical when I heard that Shore had been tapped for the *Rings* movies, and when I bought the soundtrack to *Fellowship* I was quite disappointed. It is so obviously derivative of countless superior scores, not to mention classical composers, that Jackson would have been better off with an *Excalibur*-type pastiche of Wagner and other composers. It would have been more honest, and the music would have been better too. Still, I have to hand it to Shore. His Ring and Quest themes and Elvish music are quite beautiful, and his music for the Shire has exactly the right pastoral feel. But the first movie was badly marred by the use of ominous chanting choruses (Carl Orff by way of Jerry Goldsmith) that has become such a tiresome and tasteless cliché in fantasy movies.

The music to *The Two Towers* is much better. The chorus reappears, but only in a flashback to *Fellowship*. I especially love the grand and haunting music for the people of Rohan, particularly the use of the Norwegian fiddle, although if my ears do not deceive me, a lot of it is derivative of Miklós Rózsa's brilliant score for *El Cid*. Also beautiful is "Gollum's Song" sung by Emiliana Torrini over the closing credits. And no, it is not a "pop" song.

The main reason that I found *The Two Towers* a more satisfying movie is that it is a more unified and well-rounded dramatic whole, whereas *The Fellowship of the Ring* is more episodic. *Fellowship* falls into two natural divisions. The first part sets up the quest to destroy the Ring of Power, covering more than three thousand years in which the Ring is created, lost, and found again, and ending with the formation of the Fellowship of the Ring dedicated to destroying the Ring by returning it to the fires of Mount Doom where it was forged. The second part of *Fellow-*

ship shows the beginning of the quest itself. It too is episodic. Like all myths and sagas, it seems to lack dramatic unity.

There is just one damn thing after another.

Thus, as much as I loved *Fellowship* I do admit that I glanced at my watch around two hours in. In fairness to director Peter Jackson, however, this is a fault of Tolkien's original, and Jackson actually makes *Fellowship* a more rounded dramatic whole by ending the movie with the beginning of Tolkien's second book, *The Two Towers* (and he does it by brilliantly showing up close what Tolkien only narrates at a distance).

The Two Towers takes its name from the two foci of evil in Middle Earth (Tolkien's mythic equivalent of Europe): Orthanc, the tower of Isengard, the headquarters of the evil wizard Saruman, and Barad-dûr, the fortress of the Lord of the Rings himself, Sauron, the Dark Lord of Mordor. In the film of *The Two Towers*, Jackson focuses on the destruction of the forces of Isengard. He stops short of the end of the book, wisely reserving many events from its last chapters for the third film, *The Return of the King*, which tells the story of the final victory over Sauron.

The novel *The Two Towers* suffers from being episodic as well. In part one, Tolkien cuts back and forth between the adventures of Aragorn, Legolas, and Gimli with the riders of Rohan and of Merry and Pippin with Treebeard and the Ents. These storylines climax with the defeat of the forces of Isengard on two fronts. Part two of the novel focuses on Frodo, Sam, and Gollum, but their storyline has no natural climax and simply runs on into the next book. Jackson mixes the two parts together, cutting back and forth between them, inserting the ongoing journey of Frodo and Sam into the story of the defeat of Isengard to create a very satisfying narrative that is so intelligible that even a dolt like Roger Ebert (who complained that he could not tell the characters in *Excalibur* apart) should be able to follow it.

The Two Towers does not drag. In fact, it moves very quickly. I did look at my watch after two hours, but only because I was hoping that there would be two hours more to see!

Ideologically, I loved *The Two Towers* on many levels, but two deserve special comment.

First, Jackson has lifted the story of the romance between

Aragorn and the Elf princess Arwen from one of Tolkien's appendices and written it into the movie. This romance corresponds roughly to the romance of Siegfried and Brünnhilde in Wagner's *Ring*, at least insofar as they both involve the joining of an immortal woman who loses her immortality to a mortal man.

In Jackson's hands, however, the lovers are parted. Why? For a reason that is utterly astonishing in today's culture: they are of two different races, his mortal, hers immortal; they have two different destinies; thus they are incompatible; their romance was but a dream that could never be realized. Judging from his "chemistry" with Éowyn, Aragorn is destined to marry and perpetuate his own kind. Would that more whites do the same!

Second, *The Two Towers* underscores Tolkien's strongly anti-technological and "green" politics, and it is good for people to think about these issues, particularly the most dangerous form of the denial of nature: the denial of race. Man lives at odds with nature only on borrowed time. On the other hand, we have to do justice to our own nature as well. And man's nature is not merely to adapt his needs to the environment, but to adapt the environment to his needs. I think that Bacon's principle that "Nature to be commanded must be obeyed," does justice to both concerns.

The main sources of the environmental crisis are not science, technology, and industry *per se*. Part of the problem is human ignorance and error, which can only be fixed by better science and better technology. Part of the problem is moral, namely our choice to value every featherless biped, no matter how worthless or evil, over all other living things, no matter how noble and beautiful.

But really, do we need more Africans when that means fewer lions and elephants and banyan trees? I do not value every non-human creature. I am for curing diseases and trimming the verge. But I do not value every human life either, and it is obvious that some non-human lives are more valuable than human lives. Once the world recognizes this, we can begin to make rational decisions about our impact on the natural world.

But that will require addressing another part of the problem, the political: We need a political and economic system where the best rule for the good of all—all of nature, not merely all featherless bipeds. But instead, we have democracy and capitalism, which give equal weight to the preferences of the wise and the foolish, which means rule by the worst to the detriment of all.

Tolkien seems to believe that science and technology—represented by the Ring—are inherently destructive, that there is no way to make wise use of them, so me must forswear them altogether. I hope that this is not so. I hope that we can have a technological civilization that is in harmony with nature. But if we cannot, and if the price of technological civilization is the destruction of the most beautiful and noble creatures on this Earth, then I would prefer to live without technology. And I say this fully recognizing that I would have been dead long ago were it not for modern medicine.

Americans are so self-absorbed and self-important that I am sure that somewhere they are searching for analogies between the Two Towers and America's own Twin Towers—as if America were as important as Middle Earth. So try this analogy on for size: both sets of towers epitomize the technological, industrial society that is at war with the natural order, including the racial order. Both are symbols and centers of evil. And if they cannot be reformed then they must be destroyed, destroyed utterly.

As I said in my review of *The Fellowship of the Ring*: I urge every White Nationalist to see *The Two Towers* for a glimpse, in the here and now, of the white civilization that we have lost, and that we are working to create again.

VNN, December 22, 2002

The Return of the King

It was one minute past midnight, one last time. I knew *The Return of the King* would be a great movie, and it is. The only question in my mind was, "How great?"

Return is not as good as *The Two Towers*, my favorite *Rings* movie, but it is a magnificent, moving film, that will not disappoint, and taken together the *Rings* movies are certainly the greatest movie trilogy ever made, and rank among the greatest achievements in film history.

The *Rings* movies contain not a shred of decadence or Jewish propaganda. Although the films depart from Tolkien's books in countless ways, many of them improvements, some of them needless, a few of them flaws, they remain true to Tolkien's racial vision. This is astonishing, for director Peter Jackson surely must have felt great pressure from the culture at large, and probably directly from the Jews who produced and distributed the *Rings*, to turn the films into more multiracial propaganda, like the dreadful animated versions.

Tolkien's Middle Earth is Europe, a realm of many peoples, all of whom are described in the books as white and portrayed as such in the films. Middle Earth is threatened by the forces of the Dark Lord Sauron, who dwells in the Near East, in the land of Mordor. Sauron wishes to exterminate the white peoples of Middle Earth. His tools are his orcs, hideous creatures created through the forced miscegenation of elves (who are portrayed as extremely tall, fair, Nordic white people) and goblins. His allies are Southrons and Easterlings, who are portrayed as non-whites. The analogies to the present situation of the white race, the Jewish enemy, and his non-white tools are obvious.

Sauron's greatest tool is the Ring of Power, which he forged in the heart of the volcano, Mount Doom, and into which he invested his malice, his lust for power, indeed his very life force. So when his connection to the Ring was severed, he was all but destroyed. The Ring of Power symbolizes the danger we all face when we invest ourselves too much into external things that we can lose. This is a danger in all times and places, but much more so in the possessive materialist culture of the modern-day West. More specifically, the Ring of Power symbolizes modernity: the subjugation and degradation of nature and man through the complex of science, technology, industry, and materialism. Tolkien, a true reactionary who preferred a pre-industrial, agrarian society, thought they could never be used wisely and thus must be cast away. The whole point of *Rings* trilogy is to defeat the Dark Lord by destroying the Ring.

The weakness of Middle Earth is the fact that its peoples are divided and distrustful. More than three thousand years before, they united against the threat of Mordor, and Sauron was defeated. The linchpin of the alliance was the high king of Gondor. Gondor is very much like ancient Rome: an advanced civilization built on a colossal scale and influenced by the Atlantis-like sea-kings of Númenor. In its decadence, it is very much like Byzantium or the Rome of the German Emperors of the Middle Ages. Tolkien specifically mentions that not enough children are being born, and the population of Gondor is in decline.

Unfortunately, Isildur, the last high king, who defeated Sauron, was seduced, betrayed, and killed by the power of the Ring. The throne of Gondor stands empty. Gondor is instead ruled by a hereditary house of Stewards, much like the Marshals of the Palace of Merovingian France. The present Steward, Denethor, is played by John Noble. But there is an heir to the throne: Aragorn, played by Viggo Mortensen, who claims his throne after reuniting the peoples of Middle Earth and defeating Sauron's armies. My favorite scene is when Aragorn urges his armies—and us—to "stand, men of the West!"

There are many other powerful scenes in *Return*: the lighting of the beacons of Gondor, a riveting sequence where Pippin serenades Denethor at his table while the cavalry of Gondor charges to its doom, Minas Morgul and the muster of its armies, Aragorn's meeting with a spectral army in the heart of the haunted mountain the Dwimorberg, the deaths of King Théoden and the Witch-king of Angmar. The collapse of Sauron's tower of Barad-dûr reminded me enough of the

World Trade Center that I wonder if there is an intentional message there. If so, Professor Tolkien would probably have approved.

Other scenes were not as well done. I wish there had been more poetry and drama to the reforging of the sword Narsil, which cut the Ring from Sauron's hand three thousand years before, and its presentation to Aragorn. The siege of Gondor was well done, but the battle of the Pelennor Fields lacked the dramatic pacing that made the battle of Helm's Deep in *The Two Towers* so compelling. The Pelennor battle happened so fast that it just seemed unreal. The coronation of Aragorn was somehow less moving on screen than in the book. Sam and Frodo were really too close to the soldiers marching from Minas Morgul to avoid detection. Did not one of them look six feet up and to the right? (Maybe they should have used their elven cloaks.) Did the orcs crossing the river to the Western shore of Osgiliath really expect to surprise the enemy by paddling quietly — when they were carrying torches? Denethor's death irritated me. I can believe in magic rings and Dark Lords, but I can't believe that a man on fire would jog half a mile just to plummet to his death from the most dramatic spot in the city. The same is true of Gollum's demise. Would a body sink into molten rock like that while a metal ring would float? Better to have cut directly from Gollum falling, clutching the Ring in infantile ecstasy, to the Ring glowing on the surface of the lava pool. I was also irritated by the extra conflict scenes added between Gollum, Sam, and Frodo. They added nothing to the characterization and spoiled the pacing of the Shelob sequence, which consequently lacked suspense and drama.

Many things were cut from the book. Some I did not miss. The Prince of Dol Amroth was a cipher with a swan banner and a grand name. Gorbag and Shagrat went on so long I wanted to kill them myself. The houses of healing were not necessary since we saw in the first movie that Aragorn could heal. There really were too many Minnesota good-byes. The romance of Éowyn and Faramir will probably show up in the extended version. They both deserve that happy ending. I was sad that Jackson did not include the scene where Aragorn reveals himself to Sauron in the palantír (a crystal ball that lets one see far-off things). That could have been most poetic. So too Denethor's corruption by communing with the Dark Lord through another palantír. (Interesting that the main tool of the Dark Lord's power turns out, in effect, to be television, which literally means "far-seer.") Perhaps the palantírs too will show up in the extended version. I was very sad that Tolkien's chapter on "The Scouring of the Shire" was omitted, and I don't see how it could be added back into the extended version. It brings closure to the stories of Saruman and Wormtongue and shows the truth of Frodo's vision of the Shire in the mirror of Galadriel. One tiny disappointment was the absence of the evocative phrase "elder kindred," used by Gandalf to describe himself and the elves, who at the end of the movie depart for the lands of the West along with Frodo and Bilbo, leaving men to make their own destinies.

All these quibbles must, however, be kept in perspective. Never have I anticipated a movie more than *The Return of the King*, and given the greatness of *The Two Towers* the bar was very high indeed. As I left the theater, I sighed inwardly, "Well, it's over." I had my first introduction, the beginning of what is sure to be a long love affair. But then I realized, "No, it is not over. There is still *The Hobbit*." And yes, Peter Jackson is interested in making the film.

VNN, December 18, 2003

APPENDIX:

"THE SCOURING OF THE SHIRE"

One of my favorite parts of *The Lord of the Rings* is book 6, chapter 8, "The Scouring of the Shire," the penultimate chapter of *The Return of the King*.

After the destruction of the Ring and the downfall of the Dark Lord, Frodo, Sam, Merry, and Pippin return to the Shire, only to find that it has been seized by aliens who have enslaved and robbed the hobbits and ravaged the land.

The returning veterans rouse their people to rebellion, killing many of the usurpers and driving the rest away. Then they discover who was behind it: the fallen wizard Saruman, who is banished from the Shire. Before he can leave, however, he is killed by his servant in crime, the treacherous Wormtongue, who is then felled by three hobbit arrows.

This chapter was omitted from Peter Jackson's film trilogy (as well as Ralph Bakshi's animated version), although Jackson does allude to it in two places. In *The Fellowship of the Ring*, when Frodo peers into Galadriel's mirror, he has a vision of the hobbits enslaved and the shire blighted by dark satanic mills. In the extended version of *The Return of the King*, after the fall of Isengard, Merry and Pippin discover that Saruman's storehouses contain products from the Shire, indicating some sort of contact.

But Jackson moved the deaths of Saruman and Wormtongue to the fall of Isengard. Wormtongue still kills Saruman, but he is dispatched by an arrow from Legolas. Thus when Frodo and company return to the Shire, they find it unchanged. Thus in Jackson's telling, Frodo's vision was just one possible future foreclosed by the death of Saruman at Isengard.

Still, I think it a shame that "The Scouring of the Shire" was not filmed, for it is a potent political allegory that remains relevant today. Most commentators simply note that the Scouring is based on Tolkien's personal experience of returning from the trenches of World War I to find England a changed place. (Teeming colonies of non-whites had been established, primarily to work in port cities, which led to race riots in 1919.)[1] But the Scouring goes far beyond anything in Tolkien's experiences. It is a work of imagination, a political allegory that far more closely resembles the experiences of German soldiers returning from the Great War to find a radically new, alien-dominated regime.

The Shire was subjugated as follows. After the fall of Isengard, Saruman was reduced to a wandering "beggar in the wilderness," a refugee. But when he enjoyed power, the wandering wizard developed a far-flung network reaching all the way to the Shire, where he cultivated the friendship of Lotho Pimple.

The Shire was an agrarian, autarkic society of independent small farmers and merchants. Pimple, however, was sufficiently alienated and ambitious that he wished to change this social order. He wanted more land than he could work himself, and he wanted hirelings to work it, so he could grow rich by growing cash crops for export. In short, he wanted to be a big shot with a plantation.

By means of mysterious infusions of capital from outside the Shire (obviously from Saruman) Pimple managed to target economically troubled smallholders for takeover (perhaps by loaning them money at usurious rates and then foreclosing when they could not pay), reducing them to employees on what was once their own land. Thus Pimple became a big man, styling himself Chief Shirrif and then just Chief. When Saruman and Wormtongue arrived as refugees, naturally Pimple took them in.

Having elevated the rootless and greedy Pimple to power, Saruman cozied up with the Chief and began to institute a new order. He brought in racially indeterminate aliens to intimidate and terrorize the hobbits. He also recruited hobbits of defective character — people who wanted to act big and meddle in other people's business (in the internet age, we call them trolls) — to

---

[1] http://www.heretical.com/British/riot1919.html

vastly expand the police force. This was necessary, because Saruman also vastly expanded rules and regulations in order to yoke and mulct the hobbits. Naturally there was discontent, so a vast network of spies and informants was created, as well as a courier service to swiftly convey reports and orders. Dissidents were thus easily ferreted out and imprisoned.

Society was collectivized. Private homes were replaced by ugly, cramped, ramshackle housing developments. Crops and products were seized "for fair distribution." Rationing was introduced to crush the hobbits' spirits and lower their standard of living, freeing resources to be consumed by their new overlords or to be exported for cash. Leisure was restricted and work expanded. Handcrafts, which were fine for an aesthetically refined and ecologically sustainable subsistence economy, were replaced by heavy industry to produce exports for cash.

This industry was fueled by wholesale deforestation and fouled the water and the air. But the desecration of nature went far beyond the bounds of even economic necessity, betraying a hatred of nature and beauty as such. Saruman's real goal was less to create a new world than to destroy the old.

Finally, to cement his rule, Saruman had his collaborator Pimple secretly killed once he had outlived his usefulness.

* * *

It is simply an error to reduce this all to an allegory of the endogenous rise of capitalism in England. For the role of Saruman indicates that this process was far from endogenous in the Shire. Nor was it in England, for that matter. Saruman represents an alien influence, specifically the Jewish spirit—rootless, alienated, materialistic, and ultimately nihilistic—which is incarnated both in Jewry and its extended phenotype, Calvinism and low-church Protestantism. (It was the Puritan Revolution that brought the Jews back to England.)

Yet Saruman's takeover and elimination of Pimple does not resemble anything that happened in England. But it does resemble the revolution that deposed the Kaiser, followed by various Judeo-Bolshevik *Putsches* and ultimately the Jewish-dominated

Weimar Republic.

Furthermore, Saruman's totalitarian system of spies and informants and his expropriation of small farms and seizure of their produce did not take place in England or Germany, but it did happen in Soviet Russia, leading to some of history's greatest crimes against European man. Thus "The Scouring of the Shire" is a political allegory applicable not just to England but to all forms of Jewish subversion of traditional society.

* * *

But it is also an allegory of how a people might regain control of its destiny. The hobbits have lost their freedom through salami tactics. Each day a little more of their freedom was sliced off, but not enough to cause a general rebellion, just a lot of passive grumbling, until finally, when the meaning of what was happening dawned on them, it was too late.

Frodo and company, however, returned home after a long absence, and the change hit them all at once. It did not slowly demoralize and enervate them. It made them fighting mad. And as war veterans, they knew something about fighting.

The Shire was also lost because the hobbits were disunited and fearful, ultimately because they had enjoyed a soft and easy-going lifestyle. Frodo and his comrades, however, had been tested and hardened in the crucible of war. They were not cowed by alien bullies, no matter what their stature. They immediately resolved to rally their people and scour the Shire of the usurpers. The hobbits had been long groaning under the new regime. The veterans were the spark to the tinder.

A few opening skirmishes led to a climactic battle at Bywater, which left nearly 70 of the alien interlopers dead and the rest in chains or flight. Nineteen hobbits also lay dead. The hobbits then marched to Bag End to depose Saruman and send him packing without penalty. The prisoners were also sent on their way unharmed.

These foolishly gentle policies toward murderers were justified by Frodo with effusions of moral and metaphysical claptrap that remind us that, after all, this is children's literature.

Best we ignore him when our own enemies are at our mercy.

The closest historical analogy to "The Scouring of the Shire" comes from Germany, where various *Freikorps* groups—militias of demobilized veterans—put down Judeo-Bolshevik *Putsches* in Prussia and Bavaria. Furthermore, the successor of the *Freikorps* was the NSDAP, also led and staffed by veterans, which finally put an end to the Weimar Republic.

It is a model worth contemplating today as thousands of white veterans return from a Jewish-instigated war in Iraq to face 30% unemployment in a homeland overrun and despoiled by non-white immigrants.[2] They are a constituency just waiting for a leader.

Counter-Currents/*North American New Right*,
January 3, 2012

---

[2] http://www.counter-currents.com/2011/11/america-honors-its-veterans-veteran-unemployment-passes-30/

Batman Begins

In *Batman Begins* (2005) and its sequel *The Dark Knight* (2008), director Christopher Nolan breaks with the campy style of earlier Batman films, focusing instead on character development and motivations. This makes both films psychologically dark and intellectually and emotionally compelling.

Nolan's casts are superb. I was disappointed to learn that David Boreanaz—the perfect look, in my opinion—had been cast as Batman right up until the part was given to Christian Bale. But it is hard to fault Bale's Batman. He may be too pretty. But he has the intelligence, emotional complexity, and heroic physique needed to bring Batman to life. (Past Batmans Adam West, Michael Keaton, and George Clooney were jokes, but Val Kilmer was an intriguing choice.)

Batman Begins also stars Michael Caine, Gary Oldman, Liam Neeson, Cillian Murphy, Ken Watanabe, Rutger Hauer, and Morgan Freeman as one of those brilliant black inventors and mentors for confused whites so common in science fiction. In *The Dark Knight*, Bale, Caine, Oldman, Murphy, and Freeman return, and the immortal Heath Ledger *is* the Joker.

Batman Begins falls into three parts. In the first part we cut between Bruce Wayne in China and flashbacks of the course that brought him there. I despise the cliché that passes for psychology in popular culture today, namely that a warped psyche can be traced back to a primal trauma. So I was annoyed to learn that young Bruce Wayne became obsessed with bats when he fell down a well and was swarmed by them, and that he became a crime-fighter because his wealthy parents were gunned down in front of him by a mugger. Haunted by these traumas, billionaire Bruce Wayne ended up dropping out of Princeton to immerse himself in the criminal underworld, eventually ending up in a brutal prison in Bhutan.

Wayne is released by the mysterious Mr. Ducard—played by the imposing and charismatic Liam Neeson—who oversees his training in a mysterious Himalayan fortress run by "The League of Shadows," an ancient order of warrior-ascetics led by Ra's al Ghul (Ken Watanabe). The League follows the Traditional teaching that history moves in cycles, beginning with a Golden Age and declining into a Dark Age, which then collapses and gives place to a new Golden Age. The mission of the League of Shadows is to appear when a civilization has reached the nadir of decadence and is about to fall—and then give it a push. (Needless to say, they do not have a website or a Facebook page. Nor can one join them by sending in a check.)

The League's training is both physical and spiritual. The core of the spiritual path is to confront and overcome one's deepest fears using a hallucinogen derived from a Himalayan flower. In a powerful and poetic scene of triumph, Bruce Wayne stands unafraid in the midst of a vast swarm of bats. The first time I watched this, I missed the significance of this transformation, which is an implicit critique of "trauma" psychology, for traumas are shown to be ultimately superficial compared with the heroic strength to stand in the face of the storm. It is, moreover, perfectly consistent with the conviction that nature is ultimately more powerful than nurture.

Bruce Wayne accepts the League's training but in the end rejects its mission. He thinks that decadence can be reversed. He believes in progress. He and Ducard fight. Ra's al Ghul is killed. The fortress explodes. Wayne escapes, saving Ducard's life. Then he calls for his private jet and returns to Gotham City.

In act two, Bruce Wayne becomes Batman. Interestingly enough, Batman is much closer to Nietzsche's idea of the "Superman" than the Superman character is. Superman isn't really a man to begin with. He just looks like us. His powers are just "given." But a Nietzschean superman is a man who makes himself more than a mere man. Bruce Wayne conquers nature, both his own nature and the world around him. As a man, he makes himself more than a man.

But morally speaking, Batman is no *Übermensch*, for he remains enslaved by the sentimental notion that every human life has some sort of innate value. He does not see that this morality negates the worth of his own achievement. A Batman can only be suffered if he serves his inferiors. Universal human rights—equality—innate dignity—the sanctity of every sperm: these ideas license the subordination and ultimately the destruction of everything below—or above—humanity. They are more than just a death sentence for nature, as Pentti Linkola claims. They are a death sentence for human excellence, high culture, anything in man that points above man.

Of course Batman's humanistic ethic has limits, particularly when he makes a getaway in the Batmobile, crushing and crashing police cars, blasting through walls, tearing over rooftops. Does Bruce Wayne plan to reimburse the good citizens of Gotham, or is there a higher morality at work here after all?

In act two, Batman begins to clean up Gotham City and uncovers and unravels a complex plot. In act three, we learn who is behind it: The League of Shadows. We learn that Neeson's character Ducard is the real Ra's al Ghul, and he and the League have come to a Gotham City tottering on the brink of chaos—to send it over the edge. Of course Batman saves the day, and Gotham is allowed to limp on, sliding deeper into decadence as its people lift their eyes towards the shining mirages of hope and eternal progress that seduce and enthrall their champion as well.

Batman Begins is a dark and serious movie, livened with light humor. It is dazzling to the eye. The script was co-authored by Christopher Nolan and Jewish writer-director David Goyer. There are a few politically correct touches, such as Morgan Freeman (although I find it impossible to dislike Morgan Freeman) and the little fact that one of Wayne's ancestors was an abolitionist, but nothing that really stinks.

Batman Begins touches on many of the themes that I discerned in my reviews of Guillermo del Toro's *Hellboy* and *Hellboy II* (see chapters 10 and 11 below). Again, the villains seem to subscribe to the Traditionalist, cyclical view of history; they hold that the trajectory of history is decline; they believe that we inhabit a Dark Age and that a Golden Age will dawn only when the Dark Age is destroyed; and they wish to lend their shoulders to the wheel of time. That which is falling, should be pushed. The heroes, by contrast, believe in progress. Thus they hold that a better world can be attained by building on the present one.

This is a rather elegant and absolutely radical opposition, which can be exploited to create high stakes dramatic conflict. What fight can be more compelling than the people who want to destroy the world versus the people who want to save it?

This raises the obvious question: Who in Hollywood has been reading René Guénon and Julius Evola—or, in the case of *Hellboy*, Savitri Devi and Miguel Serrano? For somebody inside the beast clearly understands that a weaponized Traditionalism is the ultimate revolt against the modern world.

Counter-Currents/*North American New Right*,
September 23, 2010

The Dark Knight

In my review of Christopher Nolan's *Batman Begins*, I argued that the movie generates a dramatic conflict around the highest of stakes: the destruction of the modern world (epitomized by Gotham City) by the Traditionalist "League of Shadows" versus its preservation and "progressive" improvement by Batman.

I also argued that Batman's transformation into a Nietzschean *Übermensch* was incomplete, for he still accepted the reigning egalitarian-humanistic ethics that devalued his superhuman striving and achievements even as he placed them in the service of the little people of Gotham.

This latent conflict between an aristocratic and an egalitarian ethic becomes explicit in Nolan's breath-taking sequel *The Dark Knight*, which is surely the greatest supervillain movie ever. (The greatest superhero movie has to be Zack Snyder's *Watchmen* [2009].)

PHILOSOPHIZING WITH DYNAMITE

The true star of *The Dark Knight* is Heath Ledger as the Joker. The Joker is a Nietzschean philosopher. In the opening scene, he borrows Nietzsche's aphorism, "Whatever doesn't kill me, makes me stronger," giving it a twist: "I believe whatever doesn't kill you, simply makes you . . . *stranger*." Following Nietzsche, who philosophized with a hammer, the Joker philosophizes with knives as well as "dynamite, gunpowder, and . . . gasoline!"

Yes, he is a criminal. A ruthless and casual mass murderer, in fact. But he believes that "Gotham deserves a better class of criminal, and I'm going to give it to them. . . . It's not about money. It's about sending a message. Everything burns." In this, the Joker is not unlike another Nietzschean philosopher, the Unabomber, who philosophized with explosives because he too wanted to send a message.

The Joker's message is the emptiness of the reigning values.

His goal is the transvaluation of values. Although he initially wants to kill Batman, he comes to see him as a kindred spirit, an alter ego: a fellow superhuman, a fellow freak, who is still tragically tied to a humanistic morality. Consider this dialogue:

> **Batman**: Then why do you want to kill me?
> **The Joker**: I don't want to kill you! What would I do without you? Go back to ripping off mob dealers? No, no, NO! No. *You . . . you . . . complete me.*
> **Batman**: You're garbage who kills for money.
> **The Joker**: Don't talk like one of them. You're not! Even if you'd like to be. To them, you're just a freak, like me! They need you right now, but when they don't, they'll cast you out, like a leper! You see, their morals, their code, it's a bad joke. Dropped at the first sign of trouble. They're only as good as the world allows them to be. I'll show you. When the chips are down, these . . . these civilized people, they'll eat each other. See, I'm not a monster. I'm just ahead of the curve.

The Joker may want to free Batman, but he is a practitioner of tough love. His therapy involves killing random innocents, then targeting somebody Batman loves.

DEATH, AUTHENTICITY, & FREEDOM

The basis of the kinship the Joker perceives between himself and Batman is not merely a matter of eccentric garb. It is their relationship to death. The Joker is a bit of an existentialist when it comes to death: "in their last moments, people show you who they really are." Most people fear death more than anything. Thus they flee from it by picturing their death as somewhere "out there," in the future, waiting for them. But if you only have one death, and it is somewhere in the future, then right now, one is immortal. And immortal beings can afford to live foolishly and inauthentically. People only become real when they face death, and they usually put that off to the very last minute.

The Joker realizes that there is something scarier than death, and that is a life without freedom or authenticity.

The Joker realizes that mortality is not something waiting for him *out there* in the future. It is something that he carries around *inside him* at all times. He does not need a *memento mori*. He feels his own heart beating.

Because he knows he can die at any moment, he *lives* every moment.

He is *ready* to die at any moment. He accepts Harvey Dent's proposal to kill him based on a coin toss. He indicates he is willing to blow himself up to deter the black gangster Gambol—and everybody believes him. He challenges Batman to run him down just to teach him a lesson.

In his mind, the Joker's readiness to die at any moment may be his license to kill at any moment.

The Joker can face his mortality, because he has learned not to fear it. Indeed, he has come to love it, for it is the basis of his inner freedom. When Batman tries to beat information out of the Joker, he simply laughs: "You have nothing, nothing to threaten me with. Nothing to do with all your strength." Batman is powerless against him, because the Joker is prepared to die.

The Joker senses, perhaps mistakenly, that Batman could attain a similar freedom.

What might be holding Batman back? Could it be his conviction of the sanctity of life? In *Batman Begins*, Bruce Wayne breaks with the League of Shadows because he refuses the final initiation: taking another man's life. Later in the movie, he refuses to kill Ra's al Ghul (although he hypocritically lets him die). In *The Dark Knight*, Batman refuses to kill the Joker. If that is Batman's hang-up, the Joker will teach him that one can only live a more-than-human life if one replaces the love of mere life with the love of liberating death.

Lessons in Transvaluation

Many of the Joker's crimes can be understood as moral experiments and lessons.

1. When the Joker breaks a pool cue and tosses it to Gambol's three surviving henchmen, telling them that he is having "tryouts" and that only one of them (meaning the survivor) can

"join our team," he is opposing their moral scruples to their survival instincts. The one with the fewest scruples or the strongest will to survive has the advantage.

2. The Joker rigs two boats to explode, one filled with criminals and the other with the good little people of Gotham. He gives each boat the detonator switch to the other one, and tells them that unless one group chooses to blow up the other by midnight, he will blow up both boats. Again, he is opposing moral scruples to survival instincts.

The results are disappointing. The good people cannot act without a vote, and when they vote to blow up the other ship, not one of them has the guts to follow through. They would rather die than take the lives of others, and it is clearly not because they have conquered their fear of death, but simply from a lack of sheer animal vitality, of will to power. Their morality has made them sick. They don't think they have the right to live at the expense of others. Or, worse still, they all live at the expense of others. This whole System is about eating one another. But none of them will own up to that fact in front of others.

Batman interprets this as a sign that people "are ready to believe in goodness," i.e., that the Joker was wrong to claim that, "When the chips are down, these . . . these civilized people, they'll eat each other." The Joker hoped to put oversocialized people back in touch with animal vitality, and he failed. From a biological point of view, eating one another is surely healthier than going passively to one's death *en masse*.

3. The Joker goes on a killing spree to force Batman to take off his mask and turn himself in. Thus Batman must choose between giving up his mission or carrying on at the cost of individual lives. If he chooses to continue, he has to regard the Joker's victims as necessary sacrifices to serve the greater good, which means that humans don't have absolute rights that trump their sacrifice for society.

4. The Joker forces Batman to choose between saving the life of Rachel Dawes, the woman he loves, or Harvey Dent, an idealistic public servant. If Batman's true aim is to serve the common good, then he should choose Dent. But he chooses Dawes because he loves her. But the joke is on him. The Joker told him

that Dawes was at Dent's location, so Batman ends up saving Dent anyway. When Batman tells the Joker he has "one rule" (presumably not to kill) the Joker responds that he is going to have to break that one rule if he is going to save one of them, because he can save one only by letting the other die.

5. As Batman races towards the Joker on the Batcycle, the Joker taunts him: "Hit me, hit me, come on, I want you to hit me." The Joker is free and ready to die at that very moment. Batman, however, cannot bring himself to kill him. He veers off and crashes. The Joker is willing to die to teach Batman simply to kill out of healthy animal anger, without any cant about rights, due process, or other moralistic claptrap.

6. Later in the film, Batman saves the Joker from falling to his death. He could have just let him die, as he did Ra's al Ghul. The Joker says:

> Oh, you. You just couldn't let me go, could you? This is what happens when an unstoppable force meets an immovable object. You are truly incorruptible, aren't you? ... You won't kill me out of some misplaced sense of self-righteousness. And I won't kill you because you're just too much fun. I think you and I are destined to do this forever.

Again, one has the sense that the Joker would have been glad to die simply to shake Batman out of his "misplaced sense of self-righteousness."

At the risk of sounding like the Riddler:

Q: What do you call a man who is willing to die to make a philosophical point?
A: A philosopher.

MATERIALISTIC VERSUS ARISTOCRATIC MORALS

Modern materialistic society is based on two basic principles: that nothing is worse than death and nothing is better than wealth. Aristocratic society is based on the principles that there are things worse than death and better than wealth. Dishonor and slavery are worse than death. And honor and freedom are better than wealth.

We have already seen that the Joker fears death less than an inauthentic and unfree life. In one of the movie's most memorable scenes, he shows his view of wealth. The setting is the hold of a ship. A veritable mountain of money is piled up. The Joker has just recovered a trove of the mob's money — for which he will receive half. Tied up on top of the pile is Mr. Lau, the money launderer who tried to abscond with it.

One of the gangsters asks the Joker what he will do with all his money. He replies: "I'm a man of simple tastes. I like dynamite, and gunpowder, and . . . gasoline." At which point his henchmen douse the money with gasoline. The Joker continues: "And you know what they all have in common? They're cheap." He then lights the pyre and addresses the gangster: "All you care about is money. Gotham deserves a better class of criminal, and I'm going to give it to them."

Aristocratic morality makes a virtue of transforming wealth into something spiritual: into honor, prestige, or beautiful and useless things. Trading wealth for spiritual goods demonstrates one's freedom from material necessity. But the ultimate demonstration of one's freedom from material goods is the simple destruction of them.

The Indians of the Pacific Northwest practice a ceremony called the "Potlatch." In a Potlatch, tribal leaders gain prestige by giving away material wealth. However, when there was intense rivalry between individuals, they would vie for honor not by giving away wealth but by destroying it.

The Joker is practicing Potlatch. Perhaps the ultimate put-down, though, is when he mentions that he is only burning *his share* of the money.

THE MAN WITH THE PLAN

Gotham's District Attorney Harvey Dent (played by Nordic archetype Aaron Eckhart) is a genuinely noble man. He is also a man with a plan. He leaves nothing up to chance, although he pretends to. He makes decisions by flipping a coin, but the coin is rigged. It has two heads.

The Joker kidnaps Harvey Dent and Rachel Dawes and rigs

them to blow up. He gives Batman the choice of saving one. He races off to save Dawes but finds Dent instead. Dawes is killed, and Dent is horribly burned. Half his face is disfigured, and one side of his coin (which was in Rachel's possession) is blackened as well. Harvey Dent has become "Two-Face."

The Joker, of course, is a man with a plan too. Truth be told, he is a criminal mastermind, the ultimate schemer. (Indeed, one of the few faults of this movie is that his elaborate schemes seem to spring up without any time for preparation.) When the Joker visits Dent in the hospital, however, he makes the following speech in answer to Dent's accusation that Rachel's death was part of the Joker's plan.

> Do I really look like a guy with a plan? You know what I am? I'm a dog chasing cars. I wouldn't know what to do with one if I caught it. You know, I just... *do* things.
>
> The mob has plans, the cops have plans.... You know, they're schemers. Schemers trying to control their little worlds. I'm not a schemer. I try to show the schemers how pathetic their attempts to control things really are.... It's the schemers that put you where you are. You were a schemer, you had plans, and look where that got you. I just did what I do best. I took your little plan and I turned it on itself. Look what I did to this city with a few drums of gas and a couple of bullets. Hmmm?
>
> You know... You know what I've noticed? Nobody panics when things go "according to plan." Even if the plan is horrifying! If, tomorrow, I tell the press that, like, a gang banger will get shot, or a truckload of soldiers will be blown up, nobody panics, because it's all "part of the plan." But when I say that one little old mayor will die, *well then everyone loses their minds!*
>
> Introduce a little anarchy. Upset the established order, and everything becomes chaos. I'm an agent of chaos. Oh, and you know the thing about chaos? It's fair!

The Joker's immediate agenda is to gaslight Harvey Dent, to turn Gotham's White Knight into a crazed killer. "Madness," he says, "is like gravity. All you need is a little push." This speech is his push, and what he says has to be interpreted with this specific aim in mind. For instance, the claim that chaos is "fair" is clearly *a propos* of Dent's use of a two-headed coin because he refuses to leave anything up to chance. (Chaos here is equivalent to chance.) Dent's reply is to propose to decide whether the Joker lives or dies based on a coin toss. The Joker agrees, and the coin comes up in the Joker's favor. We do not see what happens, but the Joker emerges unscathed and Harvey Dent is transformed into Two-Face.

THE CONTINGENCY PLAN

But the Joker's speech is not merely a lie to send Dent over the edge. In the end, the Joker really isn't a man with a plan, and the clearest proof of that is that *he stakes his life on a coin toss*. Yes, the Joker plans for all sorts of contingencies, but he knows that the best laid plans cannot eliminate contingency as such. But that's all right, for the Joker embraces contingency as he embraces death: it is a principle of freedom.

The Joker is in revolt not only against the morals of modernity, but also its metaphysics, the reigning interpretation of Being, namely that the world is ultimately transparent to reason and susceptible to planning and control. Heidegger called this interpretation of Being the *"Gestell,"* a term which connotes classification and arrangement to maximize availability, like a book in a well-ordered library, numbered and shelved so it can be located and retrieved at will. For modern man, "to be" is to be susceptible to being classified, labeled, shelved, and available in this fashion.

Heidegger regarded such a world as an inhuman hell, and the Joker agrees. When the Joker is arrested, we find that he has no DNA or fingerprints or dental records on file. He has no name, no address, no identification of any kind. His clothes are custom made, with no labels. As Commissioner Gordon says, there's "nothing in his pockets but knives and lint." Yes, the system has him, but has nothing on him. It knows nothing about him. When he escapes, they have no idea where to look. He is a book without a barcode: unclassified, unshelved, unavailable... free.

For Heidegger, the way to freedom is to meditate on the origins of the *Gestell*, which he claims are ultimately mysterious. Why did people start thinking that everything can be understood and controlled? Was the idea cooked up by a few individuals and then propagated according to a plan? Heidegger thinks not. The *Gestell* is a transformation of the *Zeitgeist* that cannot be traced back to individual thoughts and actions, but instead conditions and leads them. Its origins and power thus remain inscrutable. The *Gestell* is an "*Ereignis*," an event, a contingency.

Heidegger suggests that etymologically "*Ereignis*" also has the sense of "taking hold" and "captivating." Some translators render it "appropriation" or "enowning." I like to render it "enthrallment": The modern interpretation of Being happened, we know not why. It is a dumb contingency. It just emerged. Now it enthralls us. We can't understand it. We can't control it. It controls us by shaping our understanding of everything else. How do we break free?

The spell is broken as soon as we realize that the idea of the *Gestell*—the idea that we can understand and control everything—cannot itself be understood or controlled. The origin of the idea that all things can be understood cannot be understood. The sway of the idea that all things can be planned and controlled cannot be planned or controlled. The reign of the idea that everything is necessary, that everything has a reason, came about as sheer, irrational contingency.

The Joker seeks to break the power of the *Gestell* not merely by *meditating* on contingency, but by *acting from it*, i.e., by *being* an irrational contingency, by being an agent of chaos.

He introduces chaos into his own life by acting on whim, by just "doing things" that don't make sense, like "a dog chasing cars": staking his life on a coin toss, playing chicken with Batman, etc. When Batman tries to beat information out of the Joker, he tells him that "The only sensible way to live in this world is without rules."

Alfred the butler understands the Joker's freedom: "Some men aren't looking for anything logical, like money. They can't be bought, bullied, reasoned, or negotiated with. Some men just want to watch the world burn."

The Joker introduces chaos into society by breaking the grip of the System and its plans.

He is capable of being an agent of chaos because of his relationship to death. He does not fear it. He embraces it as a permanent possibility. He is, therefore, free. His freedom raises him above the *Gestell*, allowing him to look down on it . . . and laugh. That's why they call him the Joker.

IN ALL SERIOUSNESS

I like the Joker's philosophy. I think he is right. "But wait," some of you might say, "the Joker is a monster! Heath Ledger claimed that the Joker was 'a psychopathic, mass murdering, schizophrenic clown with zero empathy.' Surely you don't like someone like that!"

But remember, we are dealing with Hollywood here. In a "free" society we can't suppress dangerous truths altogether. So we have to be immunized against them. That's why Hollywood lets dangerous truths appear on screen, *but only in the mouths of monsters:* Derek Vinyard in *American History X*, Travis Bickle in *Taxi Driver*, Bill the Butcher in *Gangs of New York*, Ra's al Ghul in *Batman Begins*, the Joker in *The Dark Knight*, etc.

We need to learn to separate the message from the messenger, and we need to teach the millions of people who have seen this movie (at this writing, the seventh biggest film of all time) to do so as well. Once we do that, the film ceases to reinforce the system's message and reinforces ours instead. That's what I do best. I take their propaganda and turn it on itself.

What lessons can we learn from *The Dark Knight*?

Batman Begins reveals a deep understanding of the fundamental opposition between the Traditional cyclical view of history and modern progressivism, envisioning a weaponized Traditionalism (The League of Shadows) as the ultimate enemy of Batman and the forces of progress.

The Dark Knight reveals a deep understanding of the moral and metaphysical antipodes of the modern world: the Nietzschean concept of master morality and critique of egalitarian slave morality, allied with the Heideggerian concept of the *Gestell* and the power of sheer irrational contingency to break it.

The Joker weaponizes these ideas, and he exploits Batman's latent moral conflict between Nietzschean self-overcoming and his devotion to human rights and equality.

In short, somebody in Hollywood understands who the System's most radical and fundamental enemy is. They know what ideas can destroy their world. It is time we learn them too.

Let's show these schemers how pathetic their attempts to control us really are.

Counter-Currents/*North American New Right*,
September 27, 2010

The Dark Knight Rises

The Dark Knight Rises, the third and final film of Christopher Nolan's epic Batman trilogy, does not equal *The Dark Knight*—which was scarcely possible anyway—but it is a superb piece of filmmaking. It is a better film than *Batman Begins* and develops the characters and themes of both previous films into a tremendously satisfying and deeply moving conclusion.

Christian Bale, Gary Oldman, Michael Caine, Morgan Freeman, and Cillian Murphy reprise their roles from the earlier films. Michael Caine steals the film whenever he appears on screen. New cast members include ravishing minx Anne Hathaway as the Cat Woman, the hulking, charismatic Tom Hardy as Batman's nemesis Bane, Marion Cotillard as Miranda Tate/Talia, and Joseph Gordon-Leavitt (the least Jewish-looking Jew since William Shatner) as (Robin) John Blake.

Aside from Hans Zimmer's insipid and forgettable score, this is a superbly made film, artistically and technically. It would be a shame if people did not see *The Dark Knight Rises* in theaters because of a madman's shooting rampage on opening night in Aurora, Colorado. (Many of the audience members in Aurora demonstrated, by the way, that heroism is not just for the movies.) You need to see this film on the big screen. Lightning doesn't strike twice, right?

Although I will discuss isolated elements of the plot, including the epilogue, I will say only this about the plot as a whole: The League of Shadows returns to destroy Gotham, and Batman returns to stop them. What I wish to focus upon are the larger themes of the movie, particularly those that run through the whole trilogy. The continuities between *Batman Begins* and *The Dark Knight Rises* are easy to see, since the League of Shadows is Batman's opponent in both movies. The continuities between *The Dark Knight* and the rest of the series are not so obvious, but they are deep and important.

TRADITIONALISM

In *Batman Begins*, the young Bruce Wayne is rescued from a brutal prison in the Himalayan kingdom of Bhutan by Henri Ducard a.k.a. Ra's al Ghul (Arabic for "head of the demon," played by Liam Neeson), a member of the League of Shadows, a secret brotherhood of warrior-initiates whose headquarters is somewhere high in the Himalayas.

The League of Shadows believes in the Traditional view of history. History moves in cycles, and its trajectory is decline. A historical cycle begins with a Golden Age or Age of Truth (Satya Yuga) in which mankind lives in harmony with the cosmic order. As mankind falls away from truth, however, society declines through Silver and Bronze Ages to the fourth and final age: the Iron or Dark Age (Kali Yuga), which dissolves of its own corruptions, after which a new Golden Age will arise.

The purpose of the League of Shadows is to hasten the end of the Dark Age and the dawn of the next Golden Age. Thus when a civilization is falling, they appear to give it a final push into the void: Rome, Constantinople, and now Gotham. And in every case, these are not mere cities, but cities that stand for entire civilizations. Thus the League of Shadows is here to destroy nothing less than the whole modern world.

In *Batman Begins*, the League of Shadows trains Bruce Wayne as an initiate, but he rebels before his final test and flees back to Gotham, where he reinvents himself as Batman. The League, however, follows him to Gotham to destroy the city, which is rife with corruption and decadence. Batman defeats them and kills Ra's al Ghul, but in *The Dark Knight Rises*, the League of Shadows returns under new leadership to finish the job.

"DO YOU WANNA KNOW HOW I GOT THESE SCARS?"

When the League of Shadows finds Bruce Wayne, he is a young man almost at the end of the road to self-destruction. Wayne is destroying himself due to his inability to deal with the scars of his past. His primal traumas include seeing his parents murdered by a mugger, as well as an inordinate fear of bats.

In addition to rigorous physical training, the League of Shadows also involves spiritual initiation. One such exercise involves the use of a hallucinogen derived from a Himalayan flower to confront and overcome one's deepest fears.

Another exercise is to transcend the world's ruling morality — the egalitarian notion that all human beings have some sort of intrinsic value — by killing a man. We are told he is a murderer and deserving of death. But Wayne thinks that even a murderer has value and thus deserves more than mere summary justice. He has rights to due process. So Wayne balks at this test and ends up killing quite a few members of the League of Shadows in the process. But he has no trouble with that, because they are "bad" people who don't believe in due process and the American way.

When Bruce Wayne returns to Gotham, he is an incomplete initiate. He has overcome the traumas of his past, giving him superhuman courage. His training in martial arts has given him superhuman abilities. But he has not rejected egalitarian humanism. He still subjects himself to the conventional morality. He is, in short, a superhero: a superhuman being who lives to serve his inferiors out of a sentimental sense of humanity.

Now this might not be such a bad thing, if the people he served actually looked up to him and honored him as their superior. But they are egalitarians too, thus they resent their superiors, even if they are their benefactors.

In *The Dark Knight*, the Joker is a portrait of a fully achieved *Übermensch*. (Remember that Hollywood only allows superior men to appear as monsters, because to people today, they *are* monsters.) Like Batman, the Joker has overcome the scars of his past — literal scars, in the case of the Joker. When the Joker tells people how he got his scars, he spins a new story each time. As James O'Meara brilliantly suggested, this shows that the Joker has overcome his past.[1] He tells different stories because, to him, it does not matter how he got his scars. He has transcended them — and, as we shall see, everything else in his past.

---

[1] http://www.counter-currents.com/2011/03/andy-nowickis-the-columbine-pilgrim/

Unlike Batman, however, the Joker has also gone beyond egalitarian humanism. He is psychologically free from his past and morally free from the yoke of serving his inferiors. As I argued in my essay on *The Dark Knight*, the Joker's crimes need to be seen as moral experiments to break down Batman's commitment to egalitarian humanism.

The Joker has all the traits of a fully realized initiate, but he doesn't exactly seem to be a team player. But of course we don't know how the Joker came to be the way he is, because that is part of the past he has transcended.

In *The Dark Knight Rises*, eight years have passed since the death of Harvey Dent/Two-Face. Batman's final act of self-sacrifice for the city of Gotham was to accept responsibility for Two-Face's crimes in order to preserve Harvey Dent as a symbol of incorruptible commitment to justice. Batman has disappeared, but Gotham's organized crime problem has been solved by the Dent Act, which provides for the indefinite detention of criminals.

The lie has, however, taken its toll on its architects: Bruce Wayne and Commissioner Gordon. Commissioner Gordon has lost his wife and family. Bruce Wayne has hung up his Batman costume and lives in seclusion in Wayne Manor, in mourning for Rachel Dawes, who he thought was waiting for him even though she had chosen to marry Harvey Dent. Wayne Enterprises is in a shambles, defaulting on its obligations to its shareholders and the public at large.

In short, Bruce Wayne has returned to his state at the beginning of *Batman Begins*: he is destroying himself because he cannot deal with the traumas of his past, and he is dragging everyone else down with him. Wayne is not just psychologically crippled; he is also physically crippled, walking with a cane.

When the League of Shadows returns, Wayne gets a leg brace, dusts off his Batman costume, and goes out to fight them. But Alfred warns him that despite his technological crutches, he is spiritually and physically incapable of beating Bane, who fights with the strength of belief, the strength of an initiate in the League of Shadows. And Bruce Wayne is no longer an initiate.

Alfred is right. When Bane and Batman finally clash, Bane trounces Batman, twisting his spine and then casting him into a vast pit in some god-forsaken place in Central Asia. The pit is a prison. It is open to the surface, which adds to the torment of the prisoners, who can see the world above but cannot reach it. Only one person has ever managed to climb out. Many others have died trying.

In the darkness, Wayne has to physically and spiritually rebuild himself. It is a recapitulation of his original initiation with the League of Shadows. It also recapitulates the initiation of one of his opponents, who was born in the pit and eventually climbed out as a child. Wayne masters his fear again and escapes, rising from darkness to light, the cave to the real world: perennial symbols of spiritual initiation. In this case, however, Wayne masters fear not by suppressing it but by using it. By dispensing with the safety of the rope, he reactivates his fear and uses it as motive power to make the final leap.

Having been effectively re-initiated by the League of Shadows, Wayne is now able to fight and defeat them. The message could not be clearer: technology cannot make us superhuman without the underlying spiritual preparation of initiation.

INITIATION & SUPERHUMANISM

What is the connection between Nietzschean superhumanism, which is emphasized in *The Dark Knight*, and Traditionalist initiation, which is emphasized in the other two films?

I understand Traditionalism ultimately in terms of the non-dualistic interpretation of Vedanta: the height of initiation is the mystical experience of the individual soul's identity with Being, the active principle of the universe. In our ordinary human consciousness, we experience ourselves as finite beings conditioned by other finite beings, including our traumas; these are our scars. When we experience our identity with Being, however, our finite bodies are infused with the active, creative, infinite power: the source of all things. This gives the initiate the power to overcome his merely finite, conditioned self, as well as other finite beings. Thus Traditionalists have their own supermen: the yogic adepts who attain magical powers (*siddhis*) through conscious experiencing their identity with Being.

Being is one, thus it is beyond all dualities, including the duality of good and evil. Thus the initiate who achieves mystical unity with Being rises beyond good and evil. He also rises beyond egalitarianism, since there is a fundamental difference between the initiated and the uninitiated. Finally, he rises above humanism, since he realizes that individual humans have no intrinsic worth or being. We are merely roles that Being plays for a while, masks that Being assumes and then discards. And if the initiate's role in the cosmic play is to negate millions of these nullities, what's the harm in that? Being itself cannot die, and its creative power is infinite, so there's always more where they came from.

In sum, on the nondualist Vedantic model, the culmination of initiation in a mystical experience of the identity of the self with Being leads to: (1) the infusion of superhuman powers, (2) the overcoming of external conditions, including one's past, (3) a view of the world beyond all dualities, including good and evil, and (4) the overcoming of egalitarian humanism.

Batman and the Joker display some of these traits, although nothing close to the essentially magical powers ascribed to yogic adepts. Batman, of course, never goes beyond good and evil, beyond egalitarian humanism. And the Joker, who has achieved moral liberation, does not display any superpowers, although he is remarkably accomplished.

"NOTHING IN HIS POCKETS BUT KNIVES AND LINT."

When the Joker is arrested in *The Dark Knight*, Commissioner Gordon is flummoxed: they don't know who he is. They can find no DNA, fingerprint, or dental records. They don't know his name or date of birth. His clothes are custom made, with no labels. As Gordon says, "There's nothing in his pockets but knives and lint."

If the would-be superman sometimes strives to overcome and forget his past, modern society means to keep us all tied to our pasts by compiling records. Of course mere bookkeeping cannot stop the inner spiritual transformation by which man becomes superman, rising above the conditioning of his past. But we are dealing with materialists here. Your karmic records are meaningless to them. But your tax returns and internet traffic are not.

In *The Dark Knight Rises*, Selina Kyle (Cat Woman) is searching for a computer program called Clean Slate that will delete her from all existing computer records, allowing her to completely escape from her past. She craves the Joker's freedom. Batman offers to give her the program in exchange for her help. In the end, both she and Bruce Wayne seem to have used it to escape their pasts and start a new life together in Italy.

Of course, deleting all records of one's past is not the same thing as overcoming the past psychologically and existentially. That is possible only through a fundamental transformation of one's being. But once that transformation is in place, the technology sure can be useful.

"**ALL YOU CARE ABOUT IS MONEY.**"

Contempt for money is another theme common to *The Dark Knight* and *The Dark Knight Rises*. In *The Dark Knight*, the Joker demonstrates his contempt for money by burning his share of a vast fortune.

In *The Dark Knight Rises*, some of Bane's best lines deal with money. His two most spectacular public attacks are on the stock exchange and a football game (as Gregory Hood put it so memorably: the bread and circuses of the decadent American empire).[2]

In the stock exchange, one of the traders speaks to Bane as if he were a common criminal, and a moronic one at that: "We have no money here to steal." To which Bane replies, "Then why are *you* here?"

When Bane breaks a deal with a businessman who has outlived his usefulness, the businessman protests that he has paid Bane a small fortune. "And that gives you power over me?" Bane asks.

---

[2] http://www.counter-currents.com/2012/07/the-order-in-actionthe-dark-knight-rises/

Most commentators are somewhat confused about Bane's attitude toward money, because he leads a Communist-style insurrection against the rich. But there are two critical perspectives one can take on money. Figuratively speaking, one can view it from above or from below.

Those who criticize money from below are those who lack it and want it. Their primary motive is envy, which is not necessarily wrong. A hungry man has good reason to envy your bread. And he has good reason to hate you if you prefer to waste it rather than share it. The people who criticize money from below actually have a lot in common with the people they envy: all they care about is money, either getting it or keeping it.

Bane, however, criticizes money from above. His perspective is aristocratic, not egalitarian. He is an initiate, a spiritual warrior against decadence. He realizes there is something higher than money, and he feels contempt for those who are ruled by it, for those who think that money is the highest power in this world. He is, to use the Joker's phrase, "a better class of criminal."

Like the Joker, Bane is free of material concerns even as he masterfully manipulates the base, material world to fight for higher, spiritual aims. Like the Joker, Bane is not above using people who are only interested in money to further his spiritual aims. Thus Bane both makes deals with the rich and incites the envious mob to rise against them, all to hasten the destruction of Gotham.

THE GOOD LITTLE PEOPLE OF GOTHAM

In *The Dark Knight*, the Joker argues that the people of Gotham are only as good as the world allows them to be, and when the chips are down, "they'll eat each other." This sounds like a terrible insult, but from the Joker's perspective it is actually a form of optimism. Being willing to eat one another is a sign of animal vitality unrestrained by egalitarian humanist slave morality. The Joker claims that he is not a monster; he is just "ahead of the curve": meaning that he is already what the rest of Gotham would be if only they were "allowed" by society (or courageous enough to go there without society's permission).

The Joker rigs two boats to explode and gives the detonators to the people in the other boats. He tells them that if they blow up the other boat, he will let them live. If neither boat is destroyed by midnight, he will blow up both of them. One boat is filled with criminals and cops. The other is filled with the good little people of Gotham. In the end, however, neither group manages to blow up the other, and Batman prevents the Joker from destroying both.

Batman draws the false conclusion that the boats were filled with people who believe in goodness, whereas in fact they were merely too craven, decadent, and devitalized to do anything "bad," even to save their own lives. The Joker, it turns out, was a lot farther ahead of the curve than he thought.

In *The Dark Knight Rises*, Bane proves the Joker's point, but he shows that it will take nothing less than a revolutionary mob before the people of Gotham find the courage to eat each other, beginning with the rich. The revolutionary mob gives people permission to act atavistically. But beyond that, they have moral permission as well because, in the end, egalitarian altruism really is a kind of cannibal ethics.

The least convincing part of *The Dark Knight Rises* is the portrayal of the police as improbably idealistic and self-sacrificing. In *The Dark Knight*, the police force consists almost entirely of corrupt, gun-toting bureaucrats counting the days until their pensions kick in. In *The Dark Knight Rises*, Bane lures 3,000 police into the tunnels under Gotham and traps them there. When they finally break out, they charge *en masse* into battle armed only with their sidearms against Bane's heavily-armed fighters. I don't deny that it is possible to awaken such idealism, even in the most cynical public servant. But I needed to see some *reason* for such a dramatic transformation, perhaps something analogous to Bruce Wayne's transformation in his own underground prison.

Cat Woman is motivated primarily by envy of the rich, but the revolution in Gotham has left her thoroughly disgusted. She tells Batman that as soon as she finds a way out, she is leaving. She does, however, linger for personal reasons: she wants to save Batman too. She urges him to follow, telling him that he has given everything for these people. He replies "Not everything, not yet." Then he apparently commits suicide to save the city. But in the end, we learn that Bruce Wayne was not willing to give his life for Gotham. But he was willing to give up Gotham and Batman for a life of his own.

The ending is enigmatic, but as I read it, Bruce Wayne has finally arrived at a higher level of initiation. Again, he has triumphed over his past, this time entirely, and he has used Clean Slate to erase all traces of his life and Cat Woman's. He has also risen above egalitarian humanism. He no longer lives for his inferiors. He lives for himself, and he has found happiness with Cat Woman, which is an interesting change, since it means he has decided to put his happiness above the mere fact that she is a wanted criminal.

Of course, in my eyes, the fact that Bruce Wayne has apparently chosen a private life makes him inferior to Bane. Yes, Wayne has ceased to serve those who are beneath him, but merely serving oneself is inferior to serving a cause that is greater than oneself, which is what Bane did.

TRUTH OR CONSEQUENCES

One of the most important new themes introduced in *The Dark Knight Rises* is the destructiveness of lies. Gordon and Wayne are both debilitated by the burden of the lies they told to protect the reputation of Harvey Dent. Wayne is also crushed by the loss of Rachel Dawes, which is made all the more painful because Alfred chose to conceal the fact that she had chosen to leave Bruce Wayne for Harvey Dent. Finally, near the end of the movie, Robin Blake lies to a group of orphans to give them hope, even though there really wasn't any. The common denominator is that all these lies are told altruistically, to protect people, and particularly "the people," from the truth. Lies are particularly necessary in statecraft, even at its highest and most disinterested. Lies are, of course, a form of bondage to society and the past. Thus they must be rejected by those who would be free, although the initiates seem quite willing to employ deception and violence for a higher cause.

THE LEFT AS THE VANGUARD OF NIHILISM

The Dark Knight Rises is an extremely Right wing, authoritarian, fascistic movie.

First of all, in this movie, both the good guys (Wayne, Gordon) and the bad guys (the League of Shadows) are united in their belief that Gotham is corrupt and decadent. In the earlier films, the good guys clearly believed that progress was possible. Now they are just looking for excuses to retire, because society no longer has anything to offer them. They have given without reward until their idealism has been extinguished and their souls have been completely emptied. They have become burned-out shells in thankless service to their inferiors.

Second, Nolan's portrayal of the Left is utterly unsympathetic: Leftist values are shown to be nihilistic. Thus promoting Leftism is a perfect tool for those who would destroy a society.

Third, and most trivially, the uncritical portrayal of the police would surely score high on the authoritarian personality inventory, although White Nationalists are not so naïve.

* * *

The Dark Knight Rises is a remarkable movie, a fitting conclusion to a highly entertaining and deeply serious and thought-provoking trilogy. As unlikely as it may seem, these films touch upon—and vividly illustrate—issues that are at the heart of the New Right/Radical Traditionalist critique of modernity. Tens of millions of young whites are eagerly watching and analyzing these films. Thus it is important for us to use these films to communicate our ideas.

Yes, Hollywood always puts our ideas in the mouths of psychotics in order to immunize people against them. But these ideas are one reason why the villains are always more interesting than Batman, who merely comes off as a tool.

I have suggested that these movies incorporate elements from Radical Traditionalism and Nietzschean superhumanism to generate maximum dramatic tension. What conflict could be more fundamental than the one between those who wish to destroy the world and those who wish to save it? That said, I cannot help wondering if Christopher Nolan also feels some sympathy for these ideas, although of course he would deny it. But whatever Nolan's ultimate sympathies, there is no question that somebody in Hollywood knows which ideas offer the most fundamental critique of the modern world. Isn't it time for White Nationalists to learn them as well?

Counter-Currents/*North American New Right*,
July 31, 2012

Inception

I finally went to see *Inception*. I wish I had gone on its opening night. It is one of the best movies I have ever seen. *Inception* is one of the most imaginative and brilliantly plotted movies ever, and it is also one of the most thrilling and emotionally powerful. Think *Vertigo* meets *The Matrix*—but that only just begins to describe it. You have to see *Inception* on the big screen. So stop reading now, and go see this movie before it leaves the theaters.

Inception was directed by Christopher Nolan, who is also the director of a series of increasingly impressive movies: *Following* (1998), *Memento* (2000), *Insomnia* (2002), *Batman Begins* (2005), *The Prestige* (2006), and *The Dark Knight* (2008). *The Dark Knight* is a work of genius—surely the greatest supervillain movie ever. (I say "supervillain" rather than "superhero," since Heath Ledger's Joker completely upstages Batman.) But not even *The Dark Knight* prepared me for *Inception*. Indeed, one reason I hesitated to see *Inception* for so long was the conviction that Nolan could never top *The Dark Knight*. But he has.

The premise of *Inception* is that a technology has been invented that allows people to share dreams. The active dreamer is called the "architect." He is the one who constructs the dream space into which the other dreams knowingly or unknowingly enter. (Real architects seem most suited for the job, since their visual-spatial imaginations are so powerful, and dream spaces have to be constructed as labyrinths and Escher-like topological paradoxes.)

This technology, of course, has great potential for abuse, and this is precisely what the protagonist, Dom Cobb (played by Leonardo DiCaprio), and his team are doing. By abducting people into shared dreams, DiCaprio and his team can effect the "extraction" of their most closely-guarded secrets.

DiCaprio's character is, however, no mere loathsome crook. He is a man haunted by the death of his wife, a former partner in crime, and the loss of his two children. Unable to return to the US because of a warrant for his arrest, he wanders the world extracting the secrets of the rich and powerful for their rich and powerful rivals, until he is offered a job that, if completed successfully, will allow him to return home to his family. He has to perform an "inception."

One step beyond the extraction of existing ideas is the "inception" of new ideas. How does one put an idea in another person's mind so that he thinks it is his own? It has apparently never been done before, but DiCaprio promises to do it. He assembles a team and creates a three level dream: a dream within a dream within a dream. With every new level of dreaming, the experienced dream time becomes longer. In the third level, ten years can pass while one sleeps only ten hours in the real world. Below the third level is "limbo": unstructured unconsciousness where a lifetime can pass in the blink of a terrestrial eye. If a dreamer is killed in his dream, he will fall into limbo.

All this is more than mere science fiction, for Nolan uses it to generate a powerful dramatic conflict. To reclaim his life, DiCaprio must go deeper and deeper in the dream realm, yet with every level he enters, the figure of his dead wife, who is a projection of his own guilty conscience, becomes a stronger and stronger adversary.

The conflict becomes even more exquisite when we learn that the inception that will bring him home is not the first one. He has done it before, and it was ultimately the cause of his downfall and exile.

This storyline gives *Inception* a tragic dimension and an emotional power that superficially similar movies like *The Matrix* just cannot touch. *Vertigo* is the comparison that comes to mind first, and in my book, that is the highest possible praise. I will say no more about the plot, save that the ending is poetic and deeply satisfying.

There is nothing racially, culturally, or politically offensive about *Inception*. The movie takes place all over the world, so it is natural that the cast contains an Asian and an Indian, but most of the cast is White, and Nordic at that. (The actor Joseph Gordon-Levitt looks Asian, but he is actually Jewish. Maybe the Khazar hypothesis is not dead.) There is no Hollywood monkey business of racial and ethnic casting against type.

Inception is a movie for smart people. The plot is complex and imaginative, but unlike *Memento*, it is perfectly coherent and consistent. You have to be clever and focused to follow the story, but if your mind wanders a bit, there are plenty of thrills and stunning images to keep you entertained.

Inception cements Christopher Nolan, at the age of 40, as one of the cinema's great directors. I know for sure that I will not miss the opening night of his next movie. But why are you still here? See *Inception*. See it now.

Counter-Currents/*North American New Right*,
September 3, 2010

Cronos, The Devil's Backbone, & *Pan's Labyrinth*

Guillermo del Toro is a Mexican director whose films I have been watching since I learned he was directing *The Hobbit*, which is being produced by Peter Jackson, the director of *The Lord of the Rings* trilogy. As a LOTR fanatic, I wanted to get a sense of how del Toro might handle *The Hobbit*. This is the first of three reviews I hope to write on his work so far.

Del Toro's directorial debut is *Cronos* (1993), a Mexican horror film. Made on a shoestring budget, *Cronos* is enormously impressive in style and substance, though there are some problematic scenes and occasional pacing problems (it deserves a big budget remake).

Cronos is a vampire movie, with a completely fresh take on the vampire *mythos*. The movie begins in Mexico 450 years ago. An alchemist and watchmaker has been appointed to the court of the Spanish Viceroy. There he creates an intricate golden clockwork scarab, the Cronos device (such devices have become a kind of signature in del Toro's movies, particularly the *Hellboy* films).

The purpose of the Cronos device is to halt the aging process, giving its user virtual immortality. The scarab's legs clamp into one's flesh, and a stinger resembling the scythe of Cronos penetrates a vein, pumping the blood through a mysterious filtration system and conferring renewed youth and vigor and even the power to return from the dead, so long as one's heart is not pierced.

There are, however, side effects, such as sensitivity to sunlight and — you see where this is going — an insatiable thirst for human blood.

Flash forward to the present. An elderly antiques dealer, Jesús Gris (Federico Luppi) finds the Cronos device hidden in the base of a wooden statue of an angel. By accident, it becomes attached to his body, and the transformation begins to take place.

Unfortunately, there is another party who knows of the Cronos device, a wealthy industrialist named Dieter de la Guardia, a valetudinarian and hypochondriac who inhabits a fantastic sterile lair surrounded by vaporizers and statues of angels. A display case contains preserved organs removed from his body. The rest, he says, are "on the menu." (Obsessive surgical self-mutilation appears in *Hellboy* and preserved bodies in *The Devil's Backbone*.)

In spite of his misery, he wants to live forever. Having discovered the alchemist's journal and learned of the hiding place of the Cronos device, he has sent his agents to scour Mexico for antique wooden angels. (The rejects adorn his sickroom, draped in plastic tarps and suspended by their necks from chains.)

De la Guardia's agents locate the statue at Mr. Gris's shop, and de la Guardia's nephew, ironically named Angel (and in a double irony played by the brutish Ron Perlman) is dispatched to purchase it. The secret compartment, however, is empty, and Angel is redeployed to retrieve the device from Mr. Gris. Fortunately, for all the horrors of the transformation it has begun, the device gives Mr. Gris the ability to fend off Angel's attacks and protect his wife and orphaned granddaughter.

I will say no more about the plot, save that Jesús Gris remains an entirely admirable human being throughout his transformation into a monster. He is grateful for the gifts of the Cronos device, but he has the strength of character to refuse them when he realizes that he is becoming an entirely different sort of being, a being that has no interest in protecting his loved ones, indeed a being that is becoming a menace to their welfare.

Cronos is filled with suspenseful and cringe-inducing scenes as well as mordant wit. Imagine if the Coen brothers had directed a Mexican vampire movie (in fact, they should consider doing the remake). One particularly amusing touch is Ron Perlman's obsession with getting a nose job. (Perlman is a favorite actor of del Toro's, appearing also in the *Hellboy* movies and *Blade II*.)

A theme established in *Cronos* that reappears in *The Devil's Backbone* (*El espinazo del diablo*, 2001) and *Pan's Labyrinth* (*El laberinto del fauno*, 2006) is the openness of children to the supernatural.

Mr. Gris' adorable granddaughter Aurora is uniquely attuned to her grandfather's transformation, accepts it without fear, cares for him selflessly, and bravely helps him at every turn of his fight with the de la Guardias.

The Devil's Backbone and *Pan's Labyrinth* focus primarily on children and the supernatural. They also share a common setting: Spain at the end of the Civil War. *The Devil's Backbone* is set in 1939, when it was clear that Franco had won, but he had not yet established a grip on the whole country. *Pan's Labyrinth* is set in 1944, when Franco was firmly in control and only a few Communist partisans were holding out in remote locations.

The adult heroes of both movies are Communists, but the main protagonists are children who are open to and touched by the supernatural. Del Toro seems quite open himself. He is a lapsed Catholic, but that says nothing about his views of metaphysics or the spiritual in general. But this makes it hard to fathom the consistent anti-fascist, pro-Communist propaganda in these movies.

Communism and the occult seems a bad match, after all. Communism is a materialistic, rationalistic, egalitarian doctrine that denies the existence of higher realms and secret forms of knowledge available only to a few.

Fascism, however, is a good match for the occult. Its anti-rationalism (religious, romantic, mythic, and poetic) opens it to the supernatural, and its anti-egalitarianism opens it to initiatic and esoteric knowledge. (The confluence of fascism and the occult is an explicit theme of the first *Hellboy* movie, which is filled with "Esoteric Hitlerist" touches, and even appears in more recondite forms in *Hellboy II: The Golden Army* and *Blade II*.)

The Devil's Backbone is my favorite del Toro movie. It is set in an orphanage for boys run by two elderly Communists, Carmen (Marisa Paredes), an iron lady with a wooden leg, and Dr. Casares (Federico Luppi), an impotent poet in love with Carmen. The two are hiding a hoard of Republican gold and caring for the orphans of fellow Communists. As Franco's grip tightens, however, they decide they must take the gold and the children and flee to France.

But somebody has other plans: Jacinto, the caretaker of the

orphanage, who was raised there and feels enormous resentment towards Carmen and Dr. Casares. He knows of the gold and plots to steal it. Jacinto is a shockingly ruthless and brutal villain, brilliantly portrayed by the handsome Spanish actor Eduardo Noriega.

While the adults are occupied with politics and gold, the boys at the orphanage are chasing a ghost. The night a bomb fell in the courtyard of the orphanage, one of the boys went missing. When a new boy, Carlos, arrives at the orphanage, he sees the ghost of the missing boy and tries to learn the secret of his disappearance. As the movie unfolds, the two plot lines and levels of reality intersect in a shattering conclusion.

The Devil's Backbone is rated the #5 horror movie of all time by the Rotten Tomatoes website. I think it is better described as a supernatural thriller. It is not so much frightening as mysterious, unsettling, and suspenseful. The only monsters are of the all-too-human variety. There is no computer animation, no flashy special effects. The core of this movie is a poetic script and well-developed characters beautifully portrayed, filmed with the earthy colors and warm light of a painting by Velázquez.

Pan's Labyrinth is a visually dazzling movie, heavy on special effects and monsters, human as well as inhuman. A ten-year-old girl named Ofelia and her pregnant mother travel to a remote mountain outpost where her stepfather, Captain Vidal, is rooting out Communist partisans. Vidal is a terrifying villain: his methodical sadism and self-objectifying masochism are both products of superhuman willpower divorced from conscience (much like another psychopathic *Übermensch*, the Nazi Kroenen in *Hellboy*; both men transform their own bodies and tinker with clockworks with the same detachment).

While the adults are occupied with politics, Ofelia encounters fairies and a faun. The faun tells her that she may be the reincarnation of Princess Moanna of the Underground Realm. If she can prove her identity with three tests, she can return to her kingdom. Ofelia follows the faun's instructions and has some harrowing adventures while the adults remain oblivious. Again, the two lines of plot and levels of reality are brilliantly orchestrated to come together in a powerful climax.

Some viewers think that Ofelia's adventures were merely childish fantasies and wish-fulfillment. But that is a mistake. The adults in the movie think the same way, but they are wrong too. When her mother begins to sicken, the faun instructs Ofelia to use the magic of the mandrake root to heal her. She places it under her mother's bed in a bowl of milk and feeds it two drops of blood each day. The mother's health improves. However, when the mother discovers the root, she tells Ofelia that fairy tales and magic are not real and throws the root into the fire. As it writhes and screams in the flames, Ofelia's mother goes into labor and dies in childbirth.

Magic and secret realms are not the only elements of *Pan's Labyrinth* that do not accord with Communism. Ofelia, after all, is the reincarnation of a princess. She is the heiress of a kingdom, to which she struggles to return so she can take her place on the throne. The Communists, of course, repudiate monarchy and the very principle of hereditary right. At the end, when the Communists take Captain Vidal's infant son from him, the Captain asks them to pass on a legacy. The Communists reply that the child will never even know his name.

Pan's Labyrinth is a fairytale movie about a little girl, but under no circumstances should you show it to children. On both the natural and supernatural planes, it portrays brutal and terrifying violence. The violence of the film ensures that the primary audience will be adults, i.e., the very sort of people who are closed to the magical realms it tries to reveal. For all its beauty and artistry, then, *Pan's Labyrinth* is ultimately self-subverting because of fundamental incoherencies.

My conclusion is that Guillermo del Toro is a highly talented and imaginative director. He certainly has the technical and artistic skills to direct *The Hobbit*. I have, however, pointed out some deep problems with *The Devil's Backbone* and *Pan's Labyrinth*. These might not matter, of course, since *The Hobbit* is J. R. R. Tolkien's story, not Guillermo del Toro's. Still, it gives me pause.

Having arrived at this conclusion, I learned that del Toro has now bowed out of directing *The Hobbit* because of production delays, although he is still working on the script. There is some talk—and some hope—that Peter Jackson might end up directing *The Hobbit* after all. It is his destiny. A lot of us will be greatly relieved when he stops trying to dodge it.

Counter-Currents/*North American New Right*,
July 30, 2010

Hellboy

Guillermo del Toro's *Hellboy* (2004) is grounded in a highly entertaining fusion of occult history and lore—including elements of Traditionalism, Esoteric Hitlerism, and even H. P. Lovecraft's Cthulhu *mythos*—although cut and pasted and juggled around without any regard for truth.

Hellboy begins with the character's origins. In 1944, the Nazis send a secret expedition, Project Ragna Rok, to a derelict abbey on Taramagant Island off the coast of Scotland. The abbey—probably based on Rosslyn Chapel, near Edinburgh—is built on an intersection of ley lines, meaning that it is a prime location for a portal to other dimensions.

"Ragnarok" is the Nordic name for the Apocalypse that will bring the present cosmic cycle to a fiery close. The project's goal is to open a dimensional portal and release the "Ogdru Jahad," the seven dragons of the Apocalypse or gods of chaos who slumber in crystal prisons in another dimension that seems to be identical to hell (or one hell among many).

It is not clear what the Nazis' motives are. Do they think that releasing the Ogdru Jahad will merely tip the balance of the war in their favor? Or have they concluded that the war is lost and decided to destroy the world if they cannot rule it? Or perhaps destroying the world is not a second best alternative to winning the war, but their true aim all along.

I find this last interpretation most interesting, since it coheres with the branch of Traditionalism called "Esoteric Hitlerism" whose main exponents, Savitri Devi and Miguel Serrano, claimed that the goal of National Socialism was to bring about the end of the Kali Yuga and inaugurate a new Golden Age.

Whatever the Nazi agenda, the destruction of the present world and the creation of a "new Eden" (Golden Age) is the express goal of one of the central participants in Ragna Rok: Grigori Efimovich Rasputin, "the occult adviser to the Romanovs" who has returned from the other world with a bit of "the Master" (the Devil? the Ogdru Jahad?) inside him.

The project is headed by Karl Ruprecht Kroenen, "Hitler's top assassin," an SS officer, a formidable marksman and swordsman, and the head of the Thule Society. Kroenen seems rather odd at first glance. Perhaps it is the Darth Vader-esque gas mask he wears at all times.

Later, we discover that under the mask, Kroenen's unbounded Nietzschean will to self-transcendence has transformed his body into a mere machine. He began by surgically removing his eyelids and lips, then never looked back. Tin Woodsman style, he progressively replaced his organs with intricate clockwork mechanisms as the blood in his veins turned to dust. Eventually, he becomes a mere puppet of Rasputin.

A third member of Project Ragna Rok is the beautiful blonde Ilsa Hauptstein, who first appears in a black SS cap (get it?). Rasputin grants her eternal life, youth, and the power to serve him. And she does.

Rasputin succeeds in opening the portal, but before the Ogdru Jahad can be released, it is blown up by a team of vulgar American GIs (where were the Brits?) guided by Professor Trevor "Broom" Bruttenholm, who is the paranormal adviser to President Roosevelt and the head of a top secret Bureau of Paranormal Research and Defense.

Kroenen is apparently killed, but his body disappears. Ilsa disappears as well. Rasputin is sucked into the collapsing portal, and a baby boy is spewed out: a red demon with a huge stone right hand.

The GIs name him "Hellboy," Professor Broom adopts him, and he grows up to be an agent of the Bureau of Paranormal Research and Defense, which "bumps back" at the things that go bump in the night. We learn, for instance, that the Occult War came to an end in 1958 with the death of Adolf Hitler. (Little do they know.)

It all sounds ridiculous, I know. It is a testament to Guillermo del Toro's talent as a director that he took this absurd farrago and breathed it full of pure magic.

The main plot of *Hellboy* is set 60 years later, in 2004. Played by Ron Perlman, Hellboy has grown up to be a big strapping demon in the prime of life (they age differently, we are told). His colleagues at the BPRD include Abe Sapiens, a psychic fish-man who looks like the creature from the black lagoon and talks like Niles from *Frasier* because, well, his voice is dubbed by Niles from *Frasier*; Liz Sherman, a woman who (literally) bursts into flame when she gets mad (played by Selma Blair [Beitman], Ahmet Zappa's former Jewish Princess); Tom Manning, just a sweaty, pudgy, bald, priggish, passive-aggressive civil servant (Jeffrey Tambor); and the aged Professor Broom (William Hurt).

Rasputin has returned from the dead yet again, with even more of "the Master" in him. Aided by Ilsa and Kroenen, he again seeks to bring about the Apocalypse. He reveals that Hellboy is actually the Beast of the Apocalypse (Anung Un Rama). His right hand is the key to unlock the prison of the Ogdru Jahad, which he tries to force Hellboy to do. That's all I'll say about the plot. But I must add that the sets, costumes, and monsters are just wonderful.

Enjoyable though it may be, however, *Hellboy* also has a dimension of destructive propaganda.

First, there is the high-minded voice-over at the beginning and the end that raises the question: What defines a man? The answer is: A man is not defined by his origins—his race, his heredity, his cosmic destiny—but by his *choices*.

Sure, Hellboy may be the Beast of the Apocalypse. But that's just his nature, just his destiny. Nothing that can't be transformed by being raised in an environment of liberal democratic tolerance. So instead of causing the end of the world, Hellboy cheerfully spends his time fighting against various plots to bring it about.

Hellboy is such a well-"assimilated" demon that, in every aspect—his tastes, his personality, his ideals—he is just another ugly American. From hell. Talk about a melting pot!

Second, Hellboy and his team function as symbolic proxies for Jews. This claim should come as no surprise. Jews virtually created the superhero genre, first in comics then in movies, so naturally superheroes reflect Jewish sensibilities.

Superheroes are outsiders, "freaks" who have powers that make them superior to the majority. This, of course, is how Jews see themselves. As superior outsiders, superheroes, like Jews, must practice crypsis—not because they are up to anything wrong, mind you, but merely because the peasants are too stupid to understand all the benefits of having them around. The fools might launch a pogrom against their betters "just because they are different."

Of course Jews *think* of themselves as perpetual outsiders, but in today's society, they are the ultimate insiders. The top-secret, lavishly-funded, superhero-staffed Bureau of Paranormal Research and Defense serves as a symbolic proxy for the Jewish cabals buried at the heart of Western governments—such as the Pentagon's Office of Special Plans, where Jewish neocons cooked up the Iraq War.

These sorts of cabals are never that far from the popular consciousness. It is impossible to suppress all knowledge or suspicion of them. Hence the necessity of neutralizing such suspicions.

When one contemplates the exploits of Marx and Freud, Trotsky and Herzl, the Frankfurt School and the neoconservatives—not to mention George Soros and Bernie Madoff—"superheroes" is not the word that comes to mind. We are dealing with super-*villains*, who are also outsiders, superior freaks who practice crypsis and conspiracy in order to commit monstrous crimes.

To deflect the natural identification of Jews with supervillains, Jewish writers and those schooled by them tend to give supervillains very specific, non-Jewish ethnic identities. In *Hellboy* they are Nazis and . . . Russians. Rasputin, of course, is Russian. In a scene from the director's cut, Rasputin makes a deal with a nationalistic Russian general who dreams of mother Russia's glorious rebirth. The climactic scenes also take place in Russia. But this should come as no surprise, for the Russians are the new Nazis, as per neoconservative propaganda (not to mention the last Indiana Jones movie).

The existence of supervillains justifies the existence of superheroes, and superheroes—as symbolic proxies—justify the existence of Jews as powerful, conspiratorial outsiders burrowed deep inside the power structures of Western societies . . . which allows them to act like supervillains. Why? For our own good, of course. To save us from the Nazis and the Russkis and the Ogdru Jahad.

Because awareness of Jewish conspiracies can never fully be suppressed from the popular consciousness, it must be muted and shaped by linking it subconsciously to images of strange, superior, conspiratorial, but benevolent saviors.

Guillermo del Toro is Mexican (of European descent). He is a lapsed Catholic. The Hellboy character was created by comic book artist Mike Mignola (an Italian Roman Catholic), and the defining stories were worked out in collaboration with John Byrne (an unlikely Jew given his game and origins), for publication by Dark Horse Comics run by Bill Richardson (another unlikely Jew given his name and origins). Both the comics and the movie have prominent Christian, specifically Catholic, images and themes.

Yet all the same, they so faithfully reflect and advance Hollywood's Jewish cultural and political agenda that they provide an excellent case study in Jewish intellectual hegemony over non-Jews. Frankly, to me that is an "occult" phenomenon far scarier than anything hell can spit out.

Counter-Currents/*North American New Right*,
August 6, 2010

Hellboy II:
The Golden Army

Hellboy II: The Golden Army (2008) looks like Guillermo del Toro's audition for *The Hobbit*. (He got the job, but backed out because of scheduling problems with the studio.) The root mythology is Tolkienesque: In remotest antiquity, elves, trolls, and other beings shared the earth with mankind. The visual style is pure Peter Jackson: The elves look like Tolkien/Peter Jackson elves; the trolls look like Tolkien/Peter Jackson trolls; etc.

Once upon a time, the human race was locked in ceaseless war against the elves, trolls, and allied races. Seeking to end the war, the elf king Balor commissioned the creation of the Golden Army, a horde of indestructible robots. When unleashed, the Golden Army fought with such soulless, mechanical ferocity that the humans were quickly crushed and sued for peace. The elf king himself recoiled in horror at the carnage and shut down the Golden Army. The elves and their allies made a truce with men, dividing the world between them, the former claiming the natural world, the latter keeping the man-made one.

Flash forward to the present. In the modern age, we men have forgotten the truce and transgressed our bounds. With billions of mouths to feed and asses to wipe, we have assaulted and despoiled nature with asphalt and shopping malls, oil slicks and nuclear waste.

The elf prince Nuada, therefore, has decided to reactivate the Golden Army, greatly cull the human herd, bring the present Dark Age to an end, and usher in a new Eden, another Golden Age.

The Golden Army raises a very important theme, what Savitri Devi called, in a book of that name, the *Impeachment of Man*. The elves are guardians of nature, and in the present world, that calls for drastic measures. Like Finnish eco-fascist Pentti Linkola, Prince Nuada realizes that "humanism"—the idea that every human being has unconditional value—is a death sentence for nature. We must, therefore, reject humanism and cull humanity.

I was shocked that Nuada was actually given a chance to make a case for this view. Having unleashed the last "elemental" (think of Tolkien's ents) on New York City, Nuada begs Hellboy not to kill it. It is, after all, the last of its kind. And the humans it is squashing and the buildings and streets it is destroying? Well, there's always more where those came from.

Later, Nuada says that when rare creatures like him and Hellboy die, the world is poorer for it. The unspoken assumption is that there are so many human beings that, when we die, the world is better for it.

Yet, in the end, we the audience cannot really be allowed to *go* there. (In a subtle touch, del Toro's Tolkienesque elves have horribly pasty, leathery, scarred faces. Such heresies, it is clear, can never be uttered by someone as beautiful as Cate Blanchett or Orlando Bloom.)

Hellboy does not go there either. Vulgar, "assimilated" demon-American that he is, Hellboy is completely unmoved by Nuada's logic and dispatches the elemental without qualms. Then, in the movie's one scene of true poetic beauty, the dying elemental expires in clouds of pollen and carpets of lush grass, transforming a New York street into a verdant glade.

It is a shame that del Toro squanders a superb opportunity to inject depth and dramatic tension into his script. Even if Hellboy remained loyal to mankind in the end, it would have made the movie infinitely more interesting if he at least entertained some doubts.

Furthermore, such doubts would have been in keeping with another theme in the movie: the choice between love and the world. Hellboy's spouse, the psychic fire-starter Liz Sherman, gives Hellboy the choice of choosing her or his mission. His mission, of course, is to save the world. Hellboy chooses Liz. Later in the movie, Hellboy is mortally wounded. Liz encounters the Angel of Death, who tells him that Hellboy's destiny is to destroy the world. Then the angel gives her a choice: to let him die then, thus saving the world, or to save him so he can be with her. She chooses love over the world, and Hellboy's life is restored. Abe Sapiens also chooses love at the cost of the destruction of the world. He is in love with Nuada's twin sister Princess Nuala.

Allowing her to die would save the world, but he chooses love.

Furthermore, *The Golden Army* contains a scene that explicitly emphasizes the dangers superheroes face from the public they seek to serve and the consequent necessity of crypsis. Hellboy chafes against the secrecy imposed upon him by the Bureau of Paranormal Research and Defense, the top-secret government agency that employs him. He constantly flouts their desire to keep his existence hidden, even posing for photographs. After all, he is a well-assimilated demon-American who fights for the safety of his fellow citizens. Why shouldn't he get some publicity? He wants his fifteen minutes.

However, after dispatching the elemental, Hellboy returns a baby he has rescued to its mother. The mother angrily demands to know what *he* has done to the baby. The mindless crowd then turns on Hellboy, "just because he is different." Ungrateful cattle.

Frankly, I found it remarkable that the issue of the loyalty and benevolence of superheroes toward ordinary people was brought up at all, for these are the only things that separate superheroes from supervillains. And, as I have argued in my review of the first *Hellboy* movie, stressing the loyalty and benevolence of superheroes has a Jewish apologetic element.

This should be no surprise, as Jews pretty much invented the superhero genre, thus superheroes tend to function as symbolic proxies for Jews. Given that Jews are a tiny, powerful group of outsiders who have burrowed their way into the heart of our society, they prefer that we believe that they will use their power like superheroes rather than like supervillains.

In *Hellboy*, the villains are Germans and Russians. In *The Golden Army*, they are Tolkienesque elves. What is the common denominator? Tolkien's elves, of course, are hyper-Nordic. In *The Golden Army*, they speak Old Gaelic, and the Golden Army itself is hidden in the far North of Ireland. (Hollywood's customary courtesies to Irish Catholics apparently do not extend to Irish elves.)

Furthermore, the villains in both movies share a cyclical philosophy of history, believe that we inhabit the dregs of the Kali Yuga, and seek to destroy the present world to usher in a new

Golden Age. They are anti-humanists, who believe in the sacredness of the whole, rather than in the sacredness of man alone. By affirming the sacredness of the whole, they say "Yes" to the great circle of creation and destruction, good and evil. (The elemental, we are told, is both a giver and a destroyer of life. It is nature itself, where life feeds on death.)

Hellboy is the Beast of the Apocalypse, the very being who is supposed to bring about such a change. Yet he ignores his true identity and throws himself into defeating Prince Nuada and making the world safe for Walmart. He fights for America, which is the embodiment of humanism and progress, the idea that man's happiness is the good, everything that frustrates it is the evil, and that through science, technology, and liberal democracy we can steadily replace evil with good, darkness with light, hell with a dayglo, muzaked, funplex, shopping mall heaven. This is, in short, a character with enormous dramatic potential.

A potential that is squandered. These deep and dramatic themes related to humanism and loyalty and progress remain undeveloped. Thus the film lacks emotional power.

Instead, del Toro focuses on the rapid-fire delivery of strictly B and C grade movie gimmicks and gags: interminable chases and fights, lots and lots of monsters—ten *Star Wars'* cantinas worth, by my count, some of them annoyingly fake looking—and, worst of all, a whole bunch of "regular guy" relationship melodrama, the nadir of which is the most embarrassing inebriation scene since . . . Well, I don't watch the kinds of movies that depend on funny drunks, so I have no frame of reference. It is vulgar, stupid, and . . . cynical, because one really has to *work* to make a movie as bad as this.

Yes, *The Golden Army* touches on important themes. Yes, it is often visually stunning: the Angel of Death, the death of the elf king Balor, the rampage of the elemental. Yes, it introduces an amusing new character, Dr. Johann Krauss, a German who has been entirely sublimated into ectoplasm and thus must occupy a very droll mechanical suit. (As a German, of course, Dr. Krauss is an authoritarian martinet. Hellboy doesn't like him. But eventually, Krauss redeems himself by adopting American anarchic individualism.)

But the real virtues of this movie just make their betrayal all the more flagrant. It could have been so much more.

Counter-Currents/*North American New Right*,
August 20, 2010

Pulp Fiction

Quentin Tarantino's *Pulp Fiction* is one of my favorite movies. I didn't want to like it. I didn't even want to see it. Everything I'd heard made me think it would be thoroughly nihilistic and quite unpleasant. But then someone at a party described *Pulp Fiction* as a movie about "greatness of soul at the end of history," and that caught my attention, because at the time I immersed for the *n*th time in Plato's *Republic*, the core of which is an account of the human soul, as well as Alexandre Kojève's *Introduction to the Reading of Hegel*, from which Francis Fukuyama derived his "end of history" trope.

The very idea of mentioning Plato and Hegel in the same breath with Quentin Tarantino may seem absurd, but bear with me. *Pulp Fiction* is not a decadent film. It is a film about the most fundamental metaphysical and moral choices we can make—that just happens to be set in the midst of the criminal underclass of a decadent society.

The basic issue to be decided is whether to live according to material or spiritual values—to satisfy one's individual desires or to subordinate these to serve something higher: the common good, one's personal sense of honor, or a religious calling. This deep seriousness makes *Pulp Fiction* more than just clever, dark-comic nihilism. It is a genuinely great movie.

The three main characters of *Pulp Fiction* are two hit men, one black (Jules Winnfield, brilliantly played by Samuel L. Jackson) and one white (Vincent Vega, played by John Travolta), and a corrupt boxer, Butch Coolidge (Bruce Willis).

Each of these men represents a particular spiritual type, defined in terms of which part of his soul rules the others. Jules Winnfield is a spiritual man, meaning that in a conflict between spiritual and material considerations, he follows the spiritual path. Butch Coolidge is an honor-driven man, meaning that in a conflict between honor and the satisfaction of his desires (even to the point of preserving his life), he chooses honor. Vincent Vega is ruled entirely by his desires, meaning that in a conflict between his desires and honor or spiritual motives, he chooses his desires.

These types of individuals correspond to the three fundamental Indo-European social "functions"/castes as explained by Georges Dumézil and reflected in Plato's *Republic*. The spiritual man corresponds to the priestly function/caste. The honor-driven man corresponds to the warrior function/caste. The desire-ruled man corresponds to the economic function/caste.

Pulp Fiction tells the overlapping stories of these three men in a complex, non-linear fashion. The meaning of the movie becomes clearer, however, if we discuss the story in chronological order.

THE OUTLINE OF THE MOVIE

The titles in quotes are Quentin Tarantino's. The others are mine.

- **Part 1**: The Diner: Two criminals known as "Pumpkin" (Tim Roth) and "Honey Bunny" (Amanda Plummer) decide to rob a diner.
- **Part 2**: The Killing: Hit men Vincent Vega and Jules Winnfield kill several people and recover a briefcase containing contents stolen from their employer, gangster Marsellus Wallace (Ving Rhames).
- **Part 3**: "Vincent Vega and Marsellus Wallace's Wife": Vincent Vega takes Marsellus Wallace's wife Mia out for dinner and dancing.
- **Part 4**: "The Gold Watch": Boxer Butch Coolidge double-crosses Marsellus Wallace and prepares to flee town when he discovers that he has to return to his apartment to recover his father's gold watch. (The prologue of this scene is a flashback that explains the significance of the watch.)
- **Part 5**: "The Bonnie Situation": Vincent Vega and Jules Winnfield have to dispose of the body of one of their associates who is accidentally shot in their car in broad daylight.
- **Part 6**: The Diner Again: After disposing of the body, Vin-

cent and Jules decide to have breakfast at a diner, only to have their meal interrupted by Pumpkin and Honey Bunny's robbery.

THE CHRONOLOGY OF EVENTS

1. The flashback to Butch's childhood
2. The Killing
3. "The Bonnie Situation"
4. The Diner/The Diner Again
5. "Vincent Vega and Marsellus Wallace's Wife"
6. "The Gold Watch"

Pulp Fiction is set in Los Angeles and environs in the early 1990s. The movie was filmed in 1993 and released in 1994.

JULES WINNFIELD, THE SPIRITUAL MAN

Let's begin the story with the killing. It is early morning. Jules Winnfield has come to pick up Vincent Vega for a job. When we meet Vincent Vega he has just returned to Los Angeles from three years in Amsterdam.

After three years in one of Europe's greatest cities, what has rubbed off on him? Vincent's conversation focuses entirely on fast food, drink, and drugs: what the Dutch eat with their French fries, what the French call a Quarter Pounder with Cheese (Royale with Cheese—on account of the metric system), where you can buy beer, the laws governing marijuana use in Holland, etc. Vincent, as we come to learn, is not stupid. He is intelligent and witty. But he is totally ruled by his desires.

Vincent and his partner Jules Winnfield go to an apartment occupied by four young thieves, three white and one black, who have stolen a briefcase from the black gangster Marsellus Wallace, who is Vega and Winnfield's employer. The two hit men are let into the apartment by the black thief Marvin, who has betrayed his white friends to the black gangster Wallace and his black enforcer Winnfield. After recovering the briefcase, Winnfield kills two of the white thieves, sadistically toying with their leader, Brett, including shooting him in the leg and quoting the Bible at him before finishing him off. This ends Part 2, "The Killing."

The storyline resumes in Part 5, "The Bonnie Situation," when the third white, who has been hiding in the bathroom, bursts out firing a .357 Magnum. All six shots miss. Jules and Vincent then shoot the gunman, collect the briefcase, and depart with Marvin in tow.

Jules interprets the fact that the bullets missed as "divine intervention." "God came down from heaven and stopped the bullets." Vincent interprets it as merely "luck," a "freak occurrence," "this shit happens." These fundamentally different interpretations reveal fundamentally different characters. As we have already seen, Vincent is ruled by his desires. Thus it makes sense that he would interpret the event in fundamentally materialistic terms as a meaningless freak accident. Jules, by contrast, gives the event a spiritual interpretation, revealing an openness to a higher reality and thus to motives higher than the satisfaction of mere material interests.

In the getaway car, Vincent turns to Marvin for his opinion of the event. Vincent is holding his gun, pointed at Marvin. Marvin, who seems none too bright, says he has no opinion. Then Vincent blows Marvin's head off, drenching the interior of the car in blood. Vincent claims it is an accident, although he was none too pleased that Marvin had not mentioned that the third white thief was hiding in the bathroom with a "hand cannon." Still, Vincent is a rather calculating and risk-averse individual. Before the hit, he meticulously questions Jules about the number of people they are facing and keeps insisting that they should have brought shotguns. Thus intentionally killing Marvin in a car in broad daylight seems uncharacteristically reckless.

To avoid being pulled over driving a car bathed in blood, Jules drives to the nearby house of his friend Jimmy (played by Quentin Tarantino himself). Jimmy is not amused. He tells his friends that he is not in the "dead nigger storage" business. His wife Bonnie, a nurse working graveyard at a hospital, will be home in an hour, and the killers, the corpse, and the car will have to be gone. Jules calls Marsellus, who dispatches Winston

Wolf (Harvey Keitel), who apparently has some experience in these matters. The whole scene is played in a darkly comic way, wallowing in the grossness of the blood and the corpse, as well as the moral sordidness of its casual disposal. Marvin is "nobody who will be missed," and, truly, there are plenty more where he came from.

After Wolf disposes of the body and departs, "The Bonnie Situation" has been resolved, and the last part of the movie commences: Part 6, The Diner Again.

Jules and Vincent decide to have breakfast at a local diner (it truly has been a long morning). Vincent orders pancakes and bacon, Jules coffee and a muffin. When Vincent offers Jules some bacon, Jules refuses on the ground that pigs are unclean animals, to which Vincent retorts in a childish voice, "Bacon tastes *good*. Pork chops taste *good*." Again Vincent shows that he is fundamentally ruled by his desires, whereas Jules has higher standards, in this case aesthetic. (Jewish dietary laws are explicitly rejected as his motive, but spiritual men routinely codify their moral and aesthetic preferences as religious commandments.)

Then the conversation returns to the bullets that missed. Vincent again dismisses it as a freak accident. Jules again insists that it was divine intervention, a message from God. He has decided to quit "the life" — meaning the life of a killer — and "wander the earth like Kane in *Kung Fu*," getting in adventures and meeting people until God tells him he is where he ought to be. Vincent, who is immune to the spiritual and focused entirely on the material, knows exactly what people with no jobs and no money who wander the earth are. They are bums. Jules is proposing to be nothing more than a bum. Vincent, whose entire life seems to be ruled by his digestive tract, then interrupts the conversation "to take a shit."

When Vincent is in the toilet, Pumpkin and Honey Bunny launch their robbery, and the movie comes full circle. It goes quite well, until Pumpkin tries to take Marsellus' case from Jules. Jules gets the drop on him, then in an absolutely riveting speech, explains that he will not kill them because he is "in a transitional period" (transitioning out of "the life"). His brush with death has brought on "a moment of clarity." He now sees through the excuses and self-deceptions he has used to rationalize his life as a criminal. He sees that he has been nothing more than a tool of "the tyranny of evil men." He keeps the briefcase. Pumpkin and Honey Bunny depart, followed by Jules and Vincent.

At this point, the movie ends, but we are not even half-way into the story. If Tarantino had originally meant to present the movie in chronological order, Samuel L. Jackson's absolutely riveting delivery makes it easy to understand why he chose to make this the final scene. Everything after it would seem like an anticlimax.

Next in the story is Part 3, "Vincent Vega and Marsellus Wallace's Wife." Vincent and Jules, having departed the diner, arrive at a bar owned by their employer, Marsellus Wallace. The scene begins with Wallace speaking to Butch Coolidge, the boxer, but I will save my discussion of this scene until later, when I discuss "The Gold Watch." Although we do not see it happen, Jules presumably tenders his resignation and departs on his spiritual quest. We learn nothing more about his fate.

Since Jules Winnfield is now departing from the story, this is the appropriate place to explore another way in which spiritual themes play a role in *Pulp Fiction*. What is in Marsellus Wallace's briefcase? When Vincent opens the briefcase in The Killing, a golden light shines out of it. Vincent takes a drag on his cigarette and stares, transfixed. In The Diner Again, when Pumpkin demands that Jules open the briefcase, again we see a golden glow. With a look of awe on his face, Pumpkin asks: "Is that what I think it is?" Jules nods yes, then Pumpkin says, "It's beautiful."

An interpretation that I find appealing has been floating around the internet since 1994: The briefcase contains Marsellus Wallace's soul.[1] He has sold it, or it has been stolen, but in any case he wants it back. This interpretation fits in with a number of details in the movie in addition to the strange glow and the looks of awe: The combination of the briefcase is

---

[1] http://www.snopes.com/movies/films/pulp.asp

666, the Number of the Beast. Jules tells Pumpkin that the briefcase contains his boss's "dirty laundry," and indeed, Marsellus Wallace has a lot of dirty laundry, a lot of sins upon his soul.

The first thing we see of Marsellus Wallace is the back of his shaved head. At the base of his skull is a large Band-Aid. One wonders if something has been removed. It has been suggested that his soul was removed through the back of his head, although the idea apparently has no basis in myth or tradition. If Jules and Vincent were trying to recover Marsellus Wallace's soul, it would also explain why God might indeed want to intervene on their behalf. And as for the death of the four thieves: Well, they are the devil's little helpers anyway.

VINCENT VEGA: THE DESIRE-DRIVEN MAN

Although Jules Winnfield quits "the life," Vincent Vega stays in Marsellus's employ, and his next job is to take Mrs. Wallace out for a night on the town while Mr. Wallace is away.

Am I the only one to whom this does not sound like a good idea? During the opening sequence of The Killing, we learn that Marsellus' white wife Mia (Uma Thurman) is a failed actress. (She was in a pilot.) We also hear that Marsellus had another of his associates, Atwan Rockamora, thrown off a fourth-storey balcony for giving Mia a foot massage. (Those of us who on this basis suspected Tarantino of being a foot fetishist were vindicated by the *Kill Bill* movies.)

For Vincent, the first order of business in taking out his boss's wife is to buy some heroin. He goes to the house of his dealer Lance (Eric Stolz). As Vincent waits for Lance, he listens to a disquisition on body piercing from Lance's wife Jody (Rosanna Arquette). Having purchased and injected some spendy gourmet heroin, Vincent departs for the Wallace residence to pick up Mia.

We soon learn that Mia is cut from the same cloth as Vincent: she is witty, playful, and entirely dominated by her desires. Cocaine is her drug of choice, along with alcohol and cigarettes. Everything about this couple is extremely cool, from Vincent's car to their clothes, their music, their witty repartee, and their wonderful dance scene. But their most disarming traits are their sensitivity and old-fashioned manners. It is impossible to dislike Vincent and Mia. It is hard not to envy them. Their lives would be a fun vacation from our lives. This whole segment of *Pulp Fiction* does full justice to both the allure and the emptiness of their postmodern hedonism.

Mia has Vincent take her to Jack Rabbit Slim's, a '50s nostalgia restaurant in which the booths are classic cars and the waiters and waitresses dress up like '50s movie and pop stars. (The prices, however, are very much in the '90s.) Vincent sums the place up brilliantly, in one of the movie's best lines: "It's like a wax museum with a pulse." After Buddy Holly takes their order, Mia slips into the bathroom to snort some coke. After dinner, they doff their shoes then compete in, and win, the Jack Rabbit Slim's twist contest. There is a great deal of clever dialogue, but the overall impression is that Vincent and Mia have only one use for their intelligence: to accumulate novel experiences and undergo pleasant sensations.

Cut to the end of the evening. Vincent and Mia stagger back to the Wallace residence. Having eaten, drunk, danced, laughed, and shot up, Vincent's desires are now moving in a sexual direction. But first he has "to take a piss." He ducks into the bathroom to get a grip on himself. Here we see the roles of reason and morality in a desire-dominated life.

For Plato, reason is a multifaceted faculty embracing everything from induction from sense experience to calculating options and outcomes to mystical insight into transcendent truths. All human beings use reason, but only the spiritual individual accesses its highest powers. Jules Winnfield's conviction that God was sending him a message is an example of the highest, mystical function of reason, although it seems none too reasonable to the rest of us.

For desire-ruled individuals like Vincent, however, reason is merely a tool to satisfy their desires. It is empirical and calculative. Modern philosophy, no matter how rational it professes to be, tends to define reason merely as a tool for the satisfaction of desire, which makes even professed rationalists hedonists in the end.

Vincent wants to fuck Mia. (There is no point in putting a finer word on it.) This, he claims, is "a test of character," and he shows that modernity defines character, like reason, in a way that leaves desire firmly in control. Vincent would enjoy fucking Mia. But he would not enjoy the probable consequences if Marsellus finds out. (Mia denies the foot massage story, but who knows . . . ?)

Vincent does not choose against sex with Mia based on his sense of the honorable or the sacred. Rather, he masters one desire by rationally counter-posing other, greater desires: the desires to remain alive and on good terms with his boss. Thus he resolves that he is going to have a drink, say goodnight, be a perfect gentleman, then go home and jerk off.

Vincent, in short, achieves self-mastery though rational self-indulgence. Reason for Vincent means hedonistic calculus. Character means the ability to sacrifice present pleasures for future pleasures. These are the highest virtues to which a hedonist can aspire.

While Vincent is communing in the toilet with the cleverer demons of his nature, Mia is getting bored in the other room. Vincent has gallantly offered Mia his coat, which she is still wearing. In a pocket, she finds his bag of heroin. Thinking it is cocaine, she snorts some of it, sending her into an immediate overdose. When Vincent finds her—glassy-eyed, foaming at the mouth, bleeding from the nose, a grotesque parody of Man Ray's "Tears"—he panics. He is a no-doubt wanted criminal. So is his boss. So he cannot take Mia to an emergency room. Too many questions. So he drives her to the house of his dealer Lance, where, after a good deal of dark-comic hysteria, he revives Mia by stabbing her in the heart with a huge syringe full of adrenaline, shocking her back to consciousness. ("Pretty trippy" chortles Jody. Then her friend Trudi celebrates life with another bong hit.)

As the bedraggled pair stumble back to the Wallace house, they no longer look so cool and attractive. They look like death warmed over. One knows that all their coolness, cleverness, and wit—not to mention what passes for reason and character in their lives—will not be enough to save them from the consequences of their affluent hedonism: addiction, degradation, and death by misadventure. (As an "anti-drug" film, *Pulp Fiction* is second only to *Requiem for a Dream*.)

POSTMODERNISM, HEDONISM, & DEATH

The story of "Vincent Vega and Marsellus Wallace's Wife" beautifully illustrates two philosophical theses: (1) there is an inner identity between postmodern culture and hedonism, and (2) hedonism, taken to an extreme, can lead to its self-overcoming by arranging an encounter with death—an encounter which, if survived, can expand one's awareness of one's self and the world to embrace non-hedonistic motives and actions.

This is not the place for a whole theory of postmodernism. "Postmodernism" is one of those academically fashionable weasel words like "paradigm" that have now seeped into middlebrow and even lowbrow discourse. Those of us who have fundamental and principled critiques of modernity quickly learned that postmodernism is not postmodern enough. Indeed, in most ways, it is just an intensification of the worst features of modernity.

For my purposes, postmodernity is an attitude toward culture characterized by (1) eclecticism or *bricolage*, meaning the mixing of different cultures and traditions, i.e., multiculturalism, and (2) irony, detachment, and playfulness toward culture, which is what allows us to mix and manipulate cultures in the first place. The opposite of multiculturalism is cultural integrity and exclusivity. The opposite of irony is earnestness. The opposite of detachment is identification. The opposite of playfulness is seriousness.

The core of a genuine culture is a worldview, an interpretation of existence and our place in it, as well as of our nature and the best form of life for us. These are *serious* matters. Because of the fundamental seriousness of a living culture, each one is characterized by a unity of style, the other side of which is an exclusion of foreign cultural forms. After all, if one takes one's own worldview seriously, one cannot take incompatible worldviews with equal seriousness. (Yes, cultures do borrow from one another, but a serious culture only borrows what it can assimilate to its own worldview and use for its greater glory.)

The core of a living culture is not primarily a set of ideas, but of *ideals*. Ideals are ideas that make *normative* claims upon us. They don't just tell us what *is*, but what *ought* to be. Like Rilke's "Archaic Torso of Apollo," ideals demand that we change our lives. The core of a living culture is a pantheon of ideals that is experienced as *numinous* and *enthralling*. An individual formed by a living culture has a fundamental sense of identification with and participation in his culture. He cannot separate himself from it, and since it is the source of his ideas of his nature, the good life, the cosmos, and his place in it, his attitude toward culture is fundamentally earnest and serious, even pious. In a very deep sense, he does not own his culture, he is owned by it.

In terms of their relationship to culture, human beings fall into two basic categories: healthy and unhealthy. Healthy human beings experience the ideals that define a culture as a challenge, as a tonic. The gap between the ideal and the real is bridged by a longing of the soul for perfection. This longing is a tension, like the tension of the bowstring or the lyre, that makes human greatness possible. Culture forms human beings not merely by evoking idealistic longings, but also by suppressing, shaping, stylizing, and sublimating our natural desires. Culture has an element of mortification. But healthy organisms embrace this ascetic dimension as a pathway to ennoblement through self-transcendence.

Unhealthy organisms experience culture in a radically different way. Ideals are not experienced as a challenge to quicken and mobilize the life force. Instead, they are experienced as a threat, an insult, an external imposition, a gnawing thorn in the flesh. The unhealthy organism wishes to free itself from the tension created by ideals—which it experiences as nothing more than unreasonable expectations (unreasonable by the standards of an immanentized reason, a mere hedonistic calculus). The unhealthy organism does not wish to suppress and sublimate his natural desires. He wishes to validate them as good enough and then express them. He wants to give them free reign, not pull back on the bit.

Unfortunately, the decadent have Will to Power too. Thus they have been able to free themselves and their desires from the tyranny of normative culture and institute a decadent counter-culture in its place. This is the true meaning of "postmodernism." Postmodernism replaces participation with detachment, earnestness with irony, seriousness with playfulness, enthrallment with emancipation. Such attitudes demythologize and profane the pantheon of numinous ideals that is the beating heart of a living culture.

Culture henceforth becomes merely a wax museum: a realm of dead, decontextualized artifacts and ideas. When a culture is eviscerated of its defining worldview, all integrity, all unity of style is lost. Cultural integrity gives way to multiculturalism, which is merely a pretentious way of describing a shopping mall where artifacts are bought and sold, mixed and matched to satisfy emancipated consumer desires: a wax museum jumping to the pulse of commerce. This is the world of *Pulp Fiction*.

Yet, as *Pulp Fiction* also shows, even when desire becomes emancipated and sovereign, it has a tendency to dialectically overcome itself. As William Blake said, "The fool who persists in his folly will become wise." As much as hedonists wish to become mere happy animals, they remain botched human beings. The human soul still contains longings for something more than mere satiation of natural desires. These longings, moreover, are closely intertwined with these desires. For instance, merely natural desires are few and easily satisfied. But the human imagination can multiply desires to infinity. Most of these artificial desires, moreover, are for objects that satisfy a need for honor, recognition, status, not mere natural creature comforts. Hedonism is not an animal existence, but merely a perverted and profaned human existence.

If *animal* life is all about contentment, plenitude, fullness—the fulfillment of our natural desires—then a distinctly *human* mode of existence emerges when hominids mortify the flesh in the name of something higher. Hegel believed that the perforation of the flesh was the first expression of human spirit in animal existence.

This throws light on the discourse on body piercing delivered by Jody, the wife of Lance the drug dealer. Jody, it is safe to say, is about as complete a hedonist as has ever existed. Yet Jody has had her body pierced sixteen times, including her left nipple, her clitoris, and her tongue. And in each instance, she used a needle rather than a relatively quick and painless piercing gun. As she says, "That gun goes against the whole idea behind piercing."

Well then, one has to ask, "What is the whole idea behind piercing?" Yes, piercing is fashionable. Yes, it is involved with sexual fetishism. (But fetishism is not mere desire either.) Yes, it is now big business. But the phenomenon cannot merely be reduced to hedonistic self-indulgence. It hurts. And it is irreversible.

Thus, in a world of casual and meaningless self-indulgence, piercing and its first cousin tattooing are deeply significant; they are tests; they are limit experiences; they are encounters with something—something in ourselves and in the world—that transcends the economy of desire. They are re-enactments of the primal *anthropogenetic* act within the context of a decadent and dehumanizing society.

But to "mortify" the flesh means literally to kill it. Each little hole is a little death, which derives its meaning from a big death, a whole death, death itself. And it is an encounter with death itself that is truly anthropogenetic—at least potentially so.

Jules and Vincent had a brush with death, but the bullets missed. For Jules, this brought on a moment of clarity. His self-deceptions were breached, he saw his life for what it really was, and he changed it. But the experience was wasted on Vincent.

Vincent and Mia Wallace also had a brush with death. (Mia's death would surely have entailed Vincent's death.) But again, it was wasted on Vincent. (We never learn how it affected Mia.)

For Hegel, however, the truly anthropogenetic encounter with death is not a mere "near miss," but rather *an intentionally* undertaken battle to the death over honor, which is the subject of Part 4, "The Gold Watch," to which we now turn.

THE GOLD WATCH

We first encounter boxer Butch Coolidge at the beginning of Part 3, "Vincent Vega and Marsellus Wallace's Wife." The setting is a tittie bar owned by Marsellus Wallace. The time is mid-morning, so the bar is empty. Butch is a small timer near the end of his career. If he was going to make it, he would have made it already. So he is looking to scrape up some retirement money by throwing a fight. Marsellus Wallace offers him a large sum of cash to lose in the fifth round. Wallace plans to bet on Butch's opponent and clean up.

Butch accepts the deal, then Wallace dispenses a bit of advice: "Now, the night of the fight, you may feel a slight sting. That's pride fuckin' wit ya. Fuck pride! Pride only hurts, it never helps. Fight through that shit. 'Cause a year from now, when you're kickin' it in the Caribbean, you're gonna say, 'Marsellus Wallace was right.'" Butch replies, "I've got no problem with that, Mr. Wallace."

Just before Butch leaves, Vincent Vega and Jules Winnfield enter, fresh from their encounter with Pumpkin and Honey Bunny. As Butch approaches the bar, Vincent, who (as we all know) has had a really bad morning, taunts him as "palooka" and "punchy." Butch is clearly incensed but lets it drop. Apparently, his pride is well in check.

We meet Butch again in Part 4, "The Gold Watch," which begins with a flashback. It is 1972. Butch is about eight years old. He is watching TV when his mother introduces him to Captain Koons (Christopher Walken), who was in the same North Vietnamese Prisoner of War camp as Butch's father, who died there.

Captain Koons has come to keep a promise to Butch's father. He is delivering a wristwatch that was bought by Butch's great-grandfather Ryan Coolidge when he went off to fight in World War I. Twenty years later, he gave it to his son Dane Coolidge, who went off to fight in World War II as a Marine. Dane was killed at the battle of Wake Island. Knowing that he had little chance of survival, he entrusted a man named Winocki, a gunner on an Air Force transport plane, with the task of delivering his watch to his infant son whom he had never seen. The gunner kept his promise, and that same watch was on the wrist of Butch's father when he was shot down over Hanoi. To keep the watch from being confiscated, Butch's father hid it in his rectum. When he died, he entrusted it to Captain Koons, who hid it in his rectum until he was released. "And now, little man," says Captain Koons, "I give the watch to you."

As young Butch reaches out for the watch, the older Butch wakes up with a start. It is the night of the fight. His trainer opens the door: "It's time, Butch." We hear the roar of the crowd.

Cut to the aftermath of the fight. A female cabbie, Esmeralda Villa Lobos, is listening to the radio as she waits outside the arena. We hear the announcers say that the other boxer, Floyd Ray Willis (a black man, according to the script) was killed and that Butch Coolidge fled the ring. Then Butch exits the arena from a window and jumps into the cab. He has broken his deal with Marsellus Wallace and is clearly on the run. But the question is: "*Why* did he fight to win, to the point of killing the other boxer?"

The natural interpretation is that his pride got the best of him. What stirred up his pride? The most plausible answer is his dream/recollection of the story of the gold watch. After all, everything in the story is connected to honor: the three generations of his family (patriotic folk from Tennessee) who fought in America's wars, two of them giving their lives. The fact that we know that these wars were not in America's interests, and that American men were sent to their deaths by aliens and traitors, does not alter the fact that the military cultivates an ethos of honor to overcome the fear of death. Furthermore, Winocki and Captain Koons both honored their promises to deliver the gold watch to the next Coolidge heir.

Thus the watch represents honor, the honor of fighting men, a fact that is not stained but enhanced by the detail that both Butch's father and Captain Koons kept it hidden in their rectums for years. As Butch later says, his father "went through a lot" to give him that watch. What they went through commands respect.

So my initial interpretation was that Butch's honor was stirred up by the recollection of the watch, thus he went into the ring and fought, not for money, but for honor. And since he had made a deal with Marsellus Wallace to throw the fight, he was risking his life to fight for honor. And he fought all-out, killing the other boxer. So Butch seems to have proved himself to be a man ruled by honor, not by desire.

HEGEL ON THE BEGINNING OF HISTORY

The duel to the death over honor is a remarkable phenomenon. Animals duel over dominance, which ensures their access to mates. But these duels result in death only by accident, because the whole process is governed by their survival instincts, and their "egos" do not prevent them from surrendering when the fight is hopeless. The duel to the death over honor is a distinctly human thing.

Indeed, in his *Phenomenology of Spirit*, Hegel claims that the duel to the death over honor is the beginning of history—and the beginning of a distinctly human form of existence and self-consciousness.

Prehistoric man is dominated by nature: the natural world around him and the natural world within him, namely his desires. History, for Hegel, is something different. It is the process of (1) our discovery of those parts of our nature that *transcend* mere animal desire, and (2) our creation of a society in accord with our true nature.

When we fully know ourselves as more than merely natural beings and finally live accordingly, then history will be over. (History can end, because as a process of discovery and construction, it is the kind of thing that can end.) Hegel claimed that history ended with the discovery that all men are free and the creation of a society that reflects that truth.

When two men duel to the death over honor, the external struggle between them conceals an internal struggle within each of them as they confront the possibility of being ruled by two different parts of their souls: *desire*, which includes the desire for self-preservation, and *honor*, which demands recognition of our worth by others.

When our sense of honor is offended, we become angry and seek to compel the offending party to respect us. If the other party is equally offended and intransigent, the struggle can escalate to the point where life is at stake.

At this point, two kinds of human beings distinguish themselves. Those who are ruled by their honor will sacrifice their lives to preserve it. Their motto is: "Death before dishonor." Those who are ruled by their desires are more concerned to preserve their lives than their honor. They will sacrifice their honor to preserve their lives. Their motto is: "Dishonor before death."

Suppose two honorable men fight to the death. One will live, one will die, but both will preserve their honor. But what if the vanquished party begs to be spared at the last moment at the price of his honor? What if his desire to survive is stronger than his sense of honor? In that case, he will become the slave of the victor.

The man who prefers death to dishonor is a natural master. The man who prefers dishonor to death — life at any price — is a natural slave. The natural master defines himself in terms of a distinctly human self-consciousness, an awareness of his transcendence over animal desire, the survival "instinct," the whole realm of biological necessity. The natural slave, by contrast, is ruled by his animal nature and experiences his sense of honor as a danger to survival. The master uses the slave's fear of death to compel him to work.

History thus begins with the emergence of a warrior aristocracy, a two-tiered society structured in terms of the oppositions between work and leisure, necessity and luxury, nature and culture. Slaves work so that the masters can enjoy leisure. Slaves secure the necessities of life so the masters can enjoy luxuries. Slaves conquer nature so masters can create culture. In a sense, the whole realm of culture is a "luxury," since none of it is necessitated by our animal desires. But in a higher sense, it is a necessity: a necessity of our distinctly human nature to understand itself and put its stamp upon the world.

THE END OF HISTORY

Hegel had the fanciful notion that there is a necessary "dialectic" between master and slave that will lead eventually lead to universal freedom, that at the end of history, the distinction between master and slave can be abolished, that all men are potential masters.

Now, to his credit, Hegel was a race realist. He was also quite realistic about the tendency of bourgeois capitalism to turn all men into spiritual slaves. Thus his view of the ideal state, which regulates economic life and reinforces the institutions that elevate human character against the corrupting influences of modernity, differs little from fascism. So in the end, Hegel's high-flown talk about universal freedom seems unworthy of him, rather like Jefferson's rhetorical gaffe that "all men are created equal."

The true heirs to Hegel's universalism are Marx and his followers, who really believed that the dialectic would lead to universal freedom. Alexandre Kojève, Hegel's greatest 20th-century Marxist interpreter, came to believe that both Communism and bourgeois capitalism/liberal democracy were paths to Hegel's vision of universal freedom. After the collapse of communism, Kojève's pupil Francis Fukuyama declared that bourgeois capitalism and liberal democracy would create what Kojève called the "universal homogeneous state," the global political and economic order in which all men would be free.

But both capitalism and communism are essentially materialistic systems. Yes, they made appeals to idealism, but primarily to motivate their subjects to fight for them. But if one system triumphed over the other, that necessity would no longer exist, and desire would be fully sovereign. Materialism would triumph. (And so it would have, were it not for the rise of another global enemy that is spiritual and warlike rather than materialistic: Islam.)

Thus Kojève came to believe that the universal homogeneous state would not be a society in which all men are masters, i.e., a society in which honor rules over desire. Rather, it would be a world in which all men are slaves, a society in which desire rules over honor.

This is the world of Nietzsche's "Last Man," the world of C. S. Lewis's "Men without Chests" (honor is traditionally associated with the chest, just as reason is associated with the head and desire with the belly and points below). This is the postmodern world, where emancipated desire and corrosive individualism and irony have reduced all normative cultures to commodities that can be bought and sold, used and discarded.

This is the end of the path blazed by the first wave of modern philosophers: Thomas Hobbes, John Locke, David Hume, etc., all of whom envisioned a liberal order founded on the sovereignty of desire, in which reason is reduced to a technical-instrumental faculty and honor is checked or sublimated into economic competitiveness and the quest for material status symbols.

From this point of view, there is no significant difference between classical liberalism and Left liberalism. Both are based on the sovereignty of desire. Although Left liberalism is more idealistic because it is dedicated to the impossible dream of overcoming natural inequality, whereas classical liberalism, always more vulgar, unimaginative, and morally complacent, is content with mere "bourgeois" legal equality.

The great theorists of liberalism offered mankind the same deal that Marsellus Wallace offered Butch: "Fuck pride. Think of the money." And our ancestors took the deal. As Marsellus hands Butch the cash, he pauses to ask, "Are you my nigger?" "It certainly appears so," Butch answers, then takes the money. In modernity, every man is the nigger, the spiritual slave, of any man with more money than him — to the precise extent that any contrary motives, such as pride or religious/intellectual enthusiasm, have been suppressed. (Marsellus, a black man, calls all of his hirelings niggers, but surely it gives him special pleasure to deem the white ones so.)

HISTORY BEGINS AGAIN

But history can never really end as long as it is possible for men to choose to place honor above money. And that is always possible, given that we really do seem to have the ability to choose which part of our soul is sovereign.

It is, moreover, possible as long as the examples of our ancestors, better men than ourselves, can still stir us. When Esmeralda asks Butch what his name means, he replies "I'm an American, honey, our names don't mean shit." It is one of the funniest lines of the movie, but also one of the saddest. Americans are such a sorry lot of spiritual slaves because we don't know who we are. We don't know who our ancestors are. We don't know what our names mean. So we don't have to live up to them. Or if we do know, we allow the Marsellus Wallaces of the world to bribe us into forgetting about it.

Of course "Butch" means something. It is a fighting man's name. Butch is a fighting man, from a long line of fighting men. Although he fights for money, not honor. But then, when he has reached the rock bottom of spiritual sordidness—when he sells himself as the nigger of a black gangster—he redeems himself. This is what makes Butch Coolidge seem so heroic.

But then we discover that we were completely wrong. Butch stops to make a phone call, and we learn that he has taken Marsellus's money then leaked the word that the fix was in, which tilted the odds dramatically in favor of his opponent. Then Butch bet all of Marsellus's money on himself and beat the other boxer—and he *had* to beat him, so he fought all-out and killed him—in order to win a huge payout. So Butch turns out to be a bigger crook than Marsellus Wallace. And we all know what happens to people who steal from Marsellus Wallace.

Butch meets his French girlfriend Fabienne at a cheap motel. They are cute together, and she obviously wants to have his children, explaining at length about how she wants to have a large, perfectly round potbelly. They plan to leave town the next morning, but Butch discovers that Fabienne forgot to pack his father's gold watch.

Again, Butch is faced with a conflict between honor and desire, a conflict in which his life is at stake. Honor tells him to retrieve the watch, although he knows that he will have to risk his life to do so, because Wallace will surely stake out his apartment. Desire, most eminently the desire to stay alive, tells him to take the money and run. So now we see, for real, what kind of man Butch is. He chooses honor, risking his life to retrieve the watch.

Butch cautiously returns to his apartment and retrieves the watch. Astonished at the ease, he ducks into his kitchen for a snack (he has had no breakfast). As he waits for the toaster, he is startled to see a submachine gun with a huge silencer lying on the counter. As he hefts the gun, he hears the toilet flush. The bathroom door opens, and there stands Vincent Vega, reading material in hand. The two men freeze, staring at each other. Then the toaster pops, breaking the spell, and Butch pulls the trigger, reducing Vega to a bullet-riddled corpse sprawled in the bathtub.

It could have been Jules Winnfield, but he followed his spiritual enthusiasm and left "the life." Vincent, ruled by his desires, stayed in. Vincent, ruled by his desires, mocked Butch as "palooka" and "punchy," daring him to retaliate. Which, eventually, he did. And given Vincent's character, it is singularly appropriate that Butch got the drop on him while he was "taking a shit."

Butch flees in Fabienne's Honda. As he waits at a light, Marsellus Wallace crosses the street in front of him with coffee and donuts for the stake out. When the two men recognize each other, Butch floors it, running Marsellus down. But his car is hit by oncoming traffic. When Marsellus comes to and sees Butch, injured in the wrecked Honda, he pulls out a .45 and starts firing wildly as he staggers across the street. Butch ducks into a pawnshop, and when Marsellus follows, Butch knocks him down and starts punching him furiously: "Feel that sting? That's pride, fuckin' wit ya."

Unfortunately, they have blundered into no ordinary pawnshop. Maynard, the shop-keeper gets the drop on Butch with a shotgun then knocks him out cold. When he comes to, he and Marsellus are tied to chairs in a basement dungeon with red S&M ball gags in their mouths. Maynard explains that nobody kills anyone in his place of business except himself or Zed, who is arriving presently. Zed and Maynard are two homosexual hillbilly sadists who apparently plan to rape, torture, and murder Marsellus and Butch.

When Zed and Maynard take Marsellus in the other room to reenact a scene from *Deliverance*, Butch manages to free himself. He could just sneak out, saving himself and leaving Marsellus to a well-deserved fate. But Butch can't do it. He chooses a riskier but more honorable path. He decides to rescue Marsellus. He looks around for a suitable weapon. First he hefts a claw hammer. Then a small chainsaw. Then a baseball bat. Finally, his eyes light on a samurai sword—the perfect symbol of honor.

He returns to the dungeon. Zed is raping Marsellus (who does look just like a hawg—a roasted one, complete with an apple in his mouth) while Maynard watches. Butch dispatches Maynard and taunts Zed. Marsellus, in the meantime, gets up, grabs Maynard's shotgun, and blasts Zed in the groin. At this point, Marsellus could have killed Butch as well. (Butch was very, very stupid to let Marsellus get the drop on him.)

But Marsellus responds to Butch's gallant gesture in kind. He agrees to drop his grievance against Butch if he does not tell anyone about what has happened and if he leaves L.A. never to return. I know it is unlikely. But if he got his soul back, maybe it is starting to kick in. (But not soon enough to save Zed from a "medieval" fate.)

Butch accepts the deal and roars off on Zed's chopper to meet Fabienne. They still have time to catch their train to Tennessee. And on that happy note, the story (as opposed to the movie) of *Pulp Fiction* ends.

* * *

Even its detractors admit that *Pulp Fiction* is a stylishly directed, superbly acted, darkly comic movie. I hope I have convinced you that it is a deeply serious movie as well. Yes, Quentin Tarantino is a thoroughly repulsive and nihilistic human being, and everything he directed before and since *Pulp Fiction* reflects that. (See my reviews of *Kill Bill: Vol. 1* and *Inglourious Basterds*.) But repugnant people create great art all the time, in spite of themselves. Yes, *Pulp Fiction* contains interracial couples, villainous bumbling whites, and noble, eloquent blacks. One just has to look beyond the casting to the story itself.

Pulp Fiction is only superficially anti-white. On a deeper level, it can aid us in rejecting modernity and recovering the spiritual foundations of something better.

Pulp Fiction is valuable for our cause as a critique of modernity in its final decadent phase, what Traditionalists call the Kali Yuga, Hegelians call the "end of history," and idiots celebrate as postmodernity. Philosophically speaking, modernity is the emancipation of desire from reason, honor, culture, and tradition.

Pulp Fiction takes such philosophical abstractions and pairs them with unforgettably dramatic concrete images and events. Modernity is Marsellus Wallace telling us to fuck pride, take his money, and become his nigger. Modernity is coke, smack, and Jack Rabbit Slim's. Modernity is Vincent Vega sprawled dead in a bathtub, Mia Wallace with a huge syringe stuck in her heart, and Jules Winnfield scooping up bits of brain and skull in the back seat of a blood-soaked car.

But *Pulp Fiction* does much more than just critique modernity. It also shows us an alternative. Not an alternative vision of society, but rather *the spiritual basis* of an alternative to modernity. Spiritually, modernity is the rule of desire. Part of the grip of modernity is that even people who intellectually reject it are still modern men who have no idea of how they could become anything else.

Most modern people lack the concepts necessary to think of themselves as anything more than desire-driven producer-consumers. Reason to them is just calculating options. Honor is just the narcissistic display of commodities that we are told symbolize status.

Pulp Fiction brilliantly concretizes and dramatizes the moments of decision when one chooses to be something more than a mere modern man: Jules Winnfield's choice to follow his desires or his mystical conviction that God is sending him a message; Butch Coolidge's choice to be a sneaky, bourgeois coward or a man of honor.

The spiritual man is Jules Winnfield, honestly confronting the fact that he has been lying to himself all his life, that he has been the tool of the "tyranny of evil men" (from Hobbes and Locke down to Marsellus Wallace), and instead "trying to be the shepherd." The warrior is Captain Koons keeping his word and delivering the gold watch; the warrior is Butch Coolidge descending back into hell with a samurai sword to do justice. These are the kinds of men who can start history again and deliver our people from evil.

Plato claims that society is the soul writ large. If democracy is the rule of desire writ large, then the regime that corresponds to Butch Coolidge's soul is a warrior aristocracy. The regime that corresponds to Jules Winnfield's soul is a form of theocracy in which social order is based on a transcendent metaphysical order, what Evola called the idea of the Imperium. If Tarantino had tried to show us the political big picture, he would have gotten it all terribly wrong. But what he does show, he gets dead right. Mapping out the political alternative is our job.

Counter-Currents/*North American New Right*
June 29 & July 6, 2011

Kill Bill: Vol. 1

Kill Bill: Vol. 1 is a martial arts movie, a samurai movie. Its music and style also pay homage to (or shamelessly rip off) Sergio Leone's great Spaghetti Westerns. *Kill Bill: Vol. 1* is also, we are told from the very beginning, the fourth opus by director Quentin Tarantino.

Tarantino's *Pulp Fiction* is a truly great film. *Jackie Brown* is likeable and entertaining but too damn long. I'll reserve judgment on *Reservoir Dogs*, since I have only seen it once, years ago, and I just can't force myself to watch it again. But if I did watch it again, I would probably think it is a good film, just not an enjoyable one.

Kill Bill: Vol. 1 is, from a purely technical point of view, a remarkable achievement. But I do not recommend it to anyone but fanatical film buffs. I saw this film the day it opened in October, but I am only now getting around to reviewing it. That fact alone, I think, could stand as a review.

Kill Bill: Vol. 1 is a simple revenge story told in the complex, non-linear Tarrantino style. The main character, "The Bride," played by the very beautiful, blue-eyed blonde Uma Thurman, was a member of group of freelance killers called the Deadly Viper Assassination Squad. Now that alone suffices to make her an unsympathetic character in my book, but she is the heroine of this movie.

She decides to quit the squad and get married. But the squad leader, Bill, wants her dead, so the killers descend on the small wedding chapel in El Paso and murder everyone inside. But "The Bride" — who was quite pregnant at the time — survives.

After four years in a coma, she wakes up and decides to get her revenge. In *Vol. 1*, we see her kill two squad members, a Negress played by Vivica Fox and an Oriental woman played by Lucy Liu. In *Vol. 2*, presumably, she will go after the white members of the squad, played by Darryl Hannah and Michael Madsen, as well as Bill himself, played by David Carradine.

Some of the greatest dramas of all time are revenge stories, and there are scenes in *Kill Bill: Vol. 1* that are genuinely powerful and moving. But just when you find yourself caught up in the film, just when you are starting to take it seriously, Tarantino douses your enthusiasm with a bucket of cold irony.

By "irony," I do not mean the literary trope whereby one intends the opposite of what one literally says. Nor do I mean the perverse "law" of human action by which one brings about the opposite of what intends.

Instead, by "irony" I mean a refusal to take serious things seriously, specifically a refusal of respect or allegiance to ideals, a refusal of their demand that we must elevate and transform our lives in their image, or even sacrifice our lives for their greater glory and continued sway.

By "irony," I mean the cynical pretense of having seen through the emptiness and vanity of all ideals.

Now, ironic detachment from small and silly things is healthy. But ironic detachment from great and serious things is a sign of decadence, because a healthy soul and a healthy society need ideals. Ideals are the only things that raise the human soul above the brute animality of our carnal desires.

The desires for food, security, sexual gratification, and continued existence do not set us apart from the animals. What sets us apart is our ability to give these things up for something higher. The desire to conform to a social hierarchy to ensure the satisfaction of our desires does not set us apart from wolves, apes, or even insects like ants and bees. What sets us apart is the ability to rebel in the name of ideals like liberty and justice.

Hegel saw the duel to the death over honor as man's passage from prehistory to history, from animal-like to human existence. The man who is willing to die for honor conquers his fear of death, which maintains his animal existence, to demand the proper recognition of his sense of honor, which is his idea of himself. There are other ideals besides personal honor, but it was probably the first ideal men were willing to die for. A beautiful symbol of the cult of honor is the samurai sword.

The samurai sword plays a prominent role in both *Pulp Fic-*

tion and *Kill Bill: Vol. 1*. In *Pulp Fiction*, Bruce Willis's character, the boxer Butch, is a small time crook. He accepts money from a gangster to throw a fight, leaks that he is going to throw the match and watches the odds of his winning plummet, then bets the payoff on himself, beats the other boxer to death, collects the loot, and is about to leave town . . . when he realizes that his father's watch, which has deep sentimental value, has been left behind.

He faces a moment of decision. He can leave without the watch and enjoy his loot. Or he can risk his life to go back for the watch. He chooses to go back. It is a matter of honor, and he is willing to risk his life for that. He shows that he is not just a clever animal, but a human being.

Then Butch and the gangster who is pursuing him fall into the hands of Zed and Maynard, a pair of homosexual sadists. Butch escapes. But he has another moment of decision. He can get away but abandon the gangster to rape and torture and probable death. Or he can go back and risk his life again to help the poor bastard. He chooses to go back. It is a matter of honor. Before he returns, however, he chooses his weapon. He rejects a baseball bat and a chainsaw and chooses a samurai sword. The perfect instrument for a human being, a being who is willing to risk his life over matters of honor.

I love *Pulp Fiction*, because the movie deals with the power of ideals like personal honor to raise us out of the cultural and spiritual hell created by cynicism and greed. I hate *Kill Bill: Vol. 1* because it takes the samurai duel to the death over honor and makes a mockery of it.

Irony is the dominant mode of American high- and middle-brow culture today because of our infestation with Jews. Jews are natural ironists because they are wandering parasites that inhabit their host countries but never become a part of them. They maintain their distinctness by sneering at everything their hosts take seriously. And now that they control America's mass media, they have the power to make us sneer too.

The result is predictable: detached from ideals, Americans and their culture—never too idealistic to begin with—have become ever more debased and enslaved to desires so low that they cannot even be called brutish. Brutes, after all, have natural, healthy desires that are limited and relatively easy to satisfy. There's not a lot of money to be made in that. (Although now that most of our food is thoroughly adulterated, people are willing to pay more for food that contains fewer ingredients.)

No, the real growth market is in artificial and unnatural tastes.

Now, some of these tastes are admirable. Indeed, they are the very essence of high culture. Sonnets, sculptures, and symphonies do not grow on trees. They are beautiful and, from the perspective of base utilitarianism, utterly useless. From a spiritual point of view, however, they are very useful, because learning to appreciate them elevates and deepens us. But appreciating high culture requires educated and refined tastes, and the higher the levels of education and refinement required, the fewer the people who can attain them.

If you are interested in making money, that is very bad. Since more people have bad taste than good, bad taste is where the money is. And the only things that stand in the way of the endless and profitable creation artificial desires for the tasteless, tacky, and base are high ideals, upright morals, and good taste, i.e., convictions that there are certain acts and certain pleasures that are beneath us. Once these are destroyed, there is nothing beneath us, no bottom, no limit on how low we can go, no end to the empty, trivial, and degrading things we are willing to do and see and consume.

Want a universal cultural solvent? Combine cynical ironism and capitalist greed. To accelerate the dissolution, spike with Jewish malice.

Quentin Tarantino is not a Jew. But he is the product of a thoroughly Jewed, decadent, cynical popular culture. His education seems to have consisted entirely of television and movies, like a lot of recent filmmakers, such as De Palma, Lucas, and Spielberg. All of them are talented technicians, but their personalities and tastes are shockingly immature, which is exactly what you would expect of people raised on Hollywood movies and television.

From a racial point of view, Tarantino is a disaster. He thinks Negroes quite clever. (If only they were as clever as the lines he feeds them.) He may be partly non-white, but he is probably just one of those whites so corrupted by anti-white propaganda that he has "ennobled" himself by inventing a Cherokee ancestor. If you can't overlook such things, then there is no point in seeing his movies at all.

The fact that *Pulp Fiction* is such a good film may be just a stunning, million-monkeys-banging-on-typewriters-producing-*Othello* kind of accident, but I think it is a sign of the power of genius to transcend bad education and cultural decadence. *Jackie Brown* also seemed, in its rambling and unfocused way, to straining for something higher. But with *Kill Bill: Vol. 1*, the culture seems, at last, to have overwhelmed Tarantino.

One can transcend one's cultural context through sheer genius, but to maintain that kind of transcendence one needs an alternative worldview, a critical perspective, a foundation to stand upon, and Tarantino clearly lacks that. A drowning man may break surface once or twice out of sheer self-exertion. But if he does not find something to cling to, the waters will swallow him in the end.

VNN, December 21, 2003

Inglourious Basterds

Quentin Tarantino's *Inglourious Basterds* [sic, sic] has been hyped as World War II action movie-cum-sadistic gorefest. In reality, it is a self-indulgent snorefest. I thought I would need a gin and tonic before I went in, but it turns out what I needed was a cup of coffee. Yes, there is some gore and sadism, but frankly I found myself hoping for more of it. Anything, really, to relieve the sheer boredom.

This is Quentin Tarantino's worst movie, and that is saying a lot, given how bad *Kill Bill: Vol. 1* is. *Pulp Fiction* was Tarantino's *Citizen Kane*, and it has been *The Magnificent Ambersons* ever since. If you find this review entertaining, let me assure you that it is far more entertaining than the movie itself. Nothing here should be interpreted as encouragement for you to waste your time and money on this preposterous and dull film.

Inglourious Basterds is about a team of American terrorists, consisting of seven Jews led by a gentile, Aldo "the Apache" Raine (played by Brad Pitt), who hails from Tennessee and claims to be part American Indian. The character is clearly based on Tarantino himself, since he too has an Italian name, hails from Tennessee, and claims to be part Cherokee. The mission of the Basterds is to terrify the Nazis by killing them in the most sadistic manner possible and mutilating their corpses. The dead are scalped. The survivors have swastikas carved in their foreheads.

Holocaust narratives are filled with tales of thousands of Jews herded to their doom by relative handfuls of Germans and their collaborators. Although this sheep-like behavior seems rather unlike the hyper-aggressive and unruly Jews of my acquaintance, most people accept it at face value and then wonder: What was wrong with these people? Why didn't they fight back?

Tarantino has asked the same question: "When you watch all the different Nazi movies, all the TV movies, it's sad, but isn't it also frustrating? Did everybody walk into the boxcar?

Didn't somebody do something?"

Inglourious Basterds is his answer. During World War II, the Jews needed the leadership of someone like Aldo the Apache, a mostly white man with a bit of red savage mixed in, just like the people who have churned out six million Holocaust flicks need to take direction from Quentin Tarantino. With Tarantino in charge, the war would have had a very different end, and *Inglourious Basterds* shows us how.

Should Jews be insulted by this premise? Of course they should. But the movie itself is far more insulting still. Indeed, this is probably the most anti-Semitic movie ever released by Hollywood. Tarantino's Jewish characters are one-dimensional, inhuman monsters. The Jewish Basterds are all as ugly as *Der Stürmer* cartoons. They have virtually no lines in the entire movie. All they do is skulk around, waiting for Aldo the Apache's commands to murder and torture Germans.

The most prominent of the Basterds is played by Eli Roth, just another degenerate Jewish director of repulsive horror films. Roth plays the "Bear Jew," who beats Germans to death with a baseball bat. He is the funniest thing in the entire movie, with his pouting, prissy mouth, drag queen makeup, and shiny brilliantined coiffure. Roth's large, hairy body (anyone can take steroids) looks menacing until one hears his high, hysteria-edged voice. There was laughter in the audience every time this castrated gorilla opened his mouth on screen.

Too shallow to realize that he was playing a monstrous buffoon, Roth really got into the role, praising *Inglourious Basterds* as "kosher porn" (is there any other kind?). He really gets off on fantasies of killing Nazis: "It's almost a deep sexual satisfaction of wanting to beat Nazis to death, an orgasmic feeling. My character gets to beat Nazis to death. That's something I could watch all day. My parents are very strong about Holocaust education."[1] They sound like lovely people, and I am sure they are really proud of what a successful boy Eli turned out to be.

Other Jews were equally smitten: Tarantino's producer,

---

[1] http://www.theatlantic.com/magazine/archive/2009/09/hollywoods-jewish-avenger/307619/

Lawrence Bender, told Tarantino, "As your producing partner, I thank you, and as a member of the Jewish tribe, I thank you, motherfucker, because this movie is a fucking Jewish wet dream."[2] Harvey and Bob Weinstein, the film's executive producers, also reportedly enjoyed the film's theme of Jewish revenge.

Tarantino also reported received uniformly positive reactions from his Jewish friends: "The Jewish males that I've known since I've been writing the film and telling them about it, they've just been, 'Man, I can't fucking wait for this fucking movie!'" "And they tell their dads, and they're like, 'I want to see that movie!'"[3]

If all these Jews have no objection to their tribe being portrayed as one-dimensional vengeful sadists, who am I to complain? Perhaps the shoe fits.

The most prominent Jewish character in the movie is the blonde-haired, blue-eyed Shoshanna (played by Mélanie Laurent), the daughter of a Jewish dairy farmer (that got the first laugh of the movie). Her family is massacred in 1941 by the SS, and somehow she turns up a few years later with an assumed French identity running a movie theater in Paris with her Negro lover. When her theater is chosen to premiere a new German movie in the presence of Hitler, Goebbels, Göring, Bormann, and other leading Nazis, she plans to bolt the doors and burn the place down as an act of revenge.

Shoshanna is a character of reptilian inhumanity. A young German, Fredrick Zoller (played by Daniel Brühl) is obviously smitten with her. A film enthusiast, he tries to strike up a conversation about movies. The contrast could not be clearer. He is warm, sincere, and polite. He sees her as a fellow human being and a fellow film enthusiast.

She sees him only as a racial enemy. She takes no interest in him until she discovers that he is both a film star and a war he-

---

[2] http://www.theatlantic.com/magazine/archive/2009/09/hollywoods-jewish-avenger/307619/

[3] http://www.theatlantic.com/magazine/archive/2009/09/hollywoods-jewish-avenger/307619/

ro, which she thinks she can use to her advantage. (He does not reveal these things to her initially, for he does not merely wish to impress her, but to befriend her.)

Her only flash of human emotion comes at the end of a scene in which she meets the SS man, Standartenführer Hans Landa (Christoph Waltz), who murdered her family, but it just heightens the impression that she is a cold-blooded master of deception and intrigue.

Shoshanna's inhumanity is heightened by comparison to Uma Thurman's revenge-driven character "The Bride" in the *Kill Bill* movies. The difference is not just a matter of who played the role (although Tarantino decided that as well) but of how the actresses were directed.

Hans Landa claims that he is effective at hunting Jews because he knows how they think. The meaning of this is made clear at the end of the film, when he turns out to be a traitor.

The Allies do not come off much better than the Jews. Aldo the Apache is the only American. He is a loud-mouthed, sadistic, duplicitous jackass with a hillbilly accent. Brad Pitt plays him for laughs, and he is genuinely funny. There are three Britons: the handsome German Michael Fassbender as film critic Lt. Archie Hicox, Mike Myers as General Ed Fenech, and the wreck of Rod Taylor as Winston Churchill. The first two come off as effete wankers, and Churchill might as well be Jabba the Hutt.

All of this is in strong contrast to the portrayal of the Germans, even the German traitors. First of all, they are mostly quite good-looking and sexy. (As P. J. O'Rourke said: "Nobody has *ever* had a fantasy about being tied to a bed and sexually ravished by someone dressed as a liberal.") Second, they are dignified, charming, and polite with strangers; warm, playful, and fun-loving among friends. Even though the Germans are supposed to be the bad guys, they are the only people in the film with whom most white people can readily identify themselves. This means that white audiences can only feel revulsion at the sadistic Jews who murder them.

Hitler, of course, is portrayed as a monster. He first appears wearing a cape, which is appropriate, since he is played as nothing more than a comic book villain. (Martin Wuttke is surely the ugliest Hitler ever.)

Goebbels, although he is portrayed as somewhat arrogant (like a film director, perhaps), comes off overall as warm, sincere, playful, and even a bit lovable (!). Tarantino has obviously immersed himself in German films of the era, and it is clear that he has some admiration for what Goebbels accomplished. (In a scene set in England, it is stated as plain fact that Jews run Hollywood, and Goebbels is given credit for giving them a run for their money.)

The true star of the film is Christoph Waltz, whose portrayal of Hans Landa is absolutely riveting. He is such a magnificent character that Tarantino had to turn him into a traitor in the end, otherwise he would be the true hero of the film as well.

The other star is Daniel Brühl who plays Fredrick Zoller, the young war hero who becomes smitten with Shoshanna. His character is the most likable and most tragic of the film.

Now let's examine the climax of the movie. I have no qualms about giving it away, since I don't want any of you to see it anyway. Shoshanna hosts the premiere. Hitler and all the top Nazis come to the theater. She splices her face into the fourth reel of the film. Once the fourth reel is playing, her Negro lover bars the doors to the theater. Suddenly, Shoshanna's face appears on the screen: "This is the face of Jewish vengeance!" she screams, while the Negro sets the building on fire. The kindling he uses are movies printed on highly flammable nitrite film. (Jews use movies—and Negroes—to create mass death and destruction in this country too.)

Meanwhile, two of the Jewish Basterds (including the preposterous Eli Roth), who have infiltrated the theater without knowing of Shoshanna's plot, run amok with machine guns, killing Hitler and Goebbels and other Nazis. The theater then explodes. Everybody dies, Jews and Germans alike. *Götterdämmerung*.

The climax of *Inglourious Basterds* is obviously based on the Oscar night massacre in neo-Nazi Harold Covington's novel *The Brigade*. If you don't believe me, read the novel for yourself.

The symbolism and the message could not be clearer: Jews

use movies and movie theaters as tools to destroy their enemies. And since the white people in the audience can most readily identify with the Germans, the message gets through: the Jewish movie business is a tool of hatred and vengeance directed against all white people.

Why would Quentin Tarantino make a movie about World War II in which Germans are portrayed as attractive human beings, Americans are portrayed as sadistic buffoons, Englishmen are portrayed as effete wankers, and Jews are portrayed as cold-blooded, inhuman mass murderers?

Why would Quentin Tarantino borrow plot elements from neo-Nazi Harold Covington's *The Brigade* to craft a climax for his movie? Why would he use that climax to expose the true anti-white agenda of Hollywood?

Is Quentin Tarantino a Nazi sympathizer?

Of course not. Nothing could be further from the truth. Quentin Tarantino is simply a nihilist with an unfailing instinct for finding and desecrating anything sacred. In *Pulp Fiction*—his one great movie, and his most sincere—Tarantino showed a profound grasp of the spiritual meaning of the duel to the death over honor, symbolized by the samurai sword. In *Kill Bill: Vol. 1*, he made a giant joke of it.

In *Inglourious Basterds*, Tarantino has taken the one truly sacred myth in modern Jew-dominated America—especially in modern Hollywood—namely World War II and the Holocaust, and he has desecrated it by inverting all of its core value judgments and reversing its stereotypes. In the process, he has exposed the true anti-white agenda of Hollywood. Why? Just because he can.

The fact that Quentin Tarantino could desecrate the Holocaust, expose Hollywood's agenda, and sell it back to Hollywood's Jews is a testament to his twisted genius and their shallowness and moral imbecility.

I wish *Inglourious Basterds* were a better movie, since I think that many white people would benefit from seeing it. Yes, the explicit message is that it is good for Jews and their hillbilly dupes to sadistically murder Germans (and any other enemies of the Jews, for that matter). But the largely white audience with which I saw the film did not seem terribly comfortable with this message.

Yes, they found Brad Pitt funny. He really was funny. But the sadism directed at Germans did not amuse. In the last scene of the film, where Aldo the Apache graphically carves a swastika in the forehead of Hans Landa and pronounces it "my masterpiece" — pathetically enough, this is probably Tarantino's view of the film — there was no laughter.

For the subliminal message was coming through loud and clear: we are all Germans now, and every time we turn our eyes to a movie screen we are seeing the face of Jewish vengeance.

TOQ Online, August 25, 2009

Django Unchained:
ANOTHER JEWISH WET DREAM

Quentin Tarantino's last movie, *Inglourious Basterds* (2007), tells the story of a group of American Jews who team up with a non-white (an Amerindian-white mix from Tennessee with an Italian name, like Tarantino himself), to torture, mutilate, and slaughter evil white men and women (Germans, Nazis) during World War II. *'Terds*, in short, is nothing but an elaborate fantasy of Jewish sadism and revenge. Tarantino's producer, Lawrence Bender, told him, "As your producing partner, I thank you, and as a member of the Jewish tribe, I thank you, motherfucker, because this movie is a fucking Jewish wet dream."[1]

Lovely people.

* * *

Tarantino's latest movie, *Django Unchained* (2012) tells the story of a black former slave, Django (Jamie Foxx), who is trained as a bounty hunter by an itinerant German dentist, Dr. Schultz (Christoph Waltz). Django and Schultz then try to locate and buy Django's wife Broomhilda (*sic*). Once Broomhilda is discovered, Django goes on to slaughter countless evil whites: slave owners, their sisters, toothless inbred redneck morons, slave traders, and the horses they rode in on—apparently with exploding bullets, given the geysers of blood, severed limbs, and flying entrails that, aside from inducing nausea and nervous laughter, give the film a tiresome, farcical feel.

Chattel slavery was an evil institution inflicted upon black slaves and free whites alike by America's small, sociopathic capitalist class, which included such revered "Founding Fathers" as George Washington and Thomas Jefferson, who, to

---

[1] http://www.theatlantic.com/magazine/archive/2009/09/hollywoods-jewish-avenger/307619/

advance the economic interests of their class, used a lot of high-flown twaddle about rights, freedom, and equality to get the rabble to fight and die in a war of secession from England.

When America was founded, it was an overwhelmingly racially and culturally homogeneous country, but it was never really an organic community in which social inequalities had to justify themselves by serving the common good. Instead, it was a liberal society in which individuals, who possess "rights" that trump considerations of the common good, sought to enrich themselves by means that a decent society would not have permitted, including slavery.

Ideally, America would have been a classical republican society with a broad middle class of self-employed farmers, tradesmen, craftsmen, and merchants. To prevent the loss of social and political freedom that comes when a few wealthy men end up employing masses of poor men, enterprising individuals would have been kept in check, so that there would be few employers and few employees. Capitalism and inequality would, in short, have been subordinated to the common good.

The second best option would have been the regulation of capitalism by a strong political alliance of independent smallholders and organized labor, with the aim of creating a genuinely organic republic. (The labor movement, in my opinion, is the one truly heroic chapter in American history.) Under such a system, slavery would have been abolished peacefully and bloodlessly, with compensation, as it was virtually everywhere else, and all blacks would have been repatriated to Africa to restore the racial and cultural homogeneity that are the greatest blessings and strengths of any society. Large plantations would have been split up into small, independent farms. The people from the big houses would have learned to pick their own damn cotton.

It would be wonderful to have a movie that dramatizes the true evils of slavery, and of capitalism more broadly, from a pro-worker, pro-smallholder point of view. But *Django Unchained* is not that movie.

The truth about slavery was evil enough. One does not need to exaggerate or tell lies about it. But this movie is filled with ludicrous lies and just plain indifference to the truth.

A title card informs us that the movie is set in 1858, "two years before the Civil War." The Civil War, of course, began in 1861.

In one scene, we see masked vigilantes on horseback, presumably the Ku Klux Klan, which was not founded until 1865.

When Dr. Schultz learns that Django's wife is named Broomhilda, he tells the story of Siegfried and Brünnhilde, incorporating elements of Wagner's *Der Ring des Nibelungen*, the libretto of which had been written in 1852 but circulated only among Wagner's friends. The two operas from which Dr. Schultz was borrowing, *Die Walküre* and *Siegfried*, premiered in 1870 in 1876 respectively.

At one point, we are ushered into the Cleopatra Club, a lavish brothel full of black whores. (Why would white men would prefer black whores when white whores were plentiful?) The historical Cleopatra, the seventh of her name, may have been a bit of a whore, but she was a Macedonian Greek, not a black.

The Cleopatra Club is decorated with busts of Queen Nefertiti, who lived 1,300 years before Cleopatra, and who was not black either. The particular bust that is reproduced, which is in the Ägyptisches Museum, Berlin, was unearthed at Tel-el-Amarna in 1912.

But why be pedantic, given that this movie is created by a consummate cynic for an audience of morons?

In one of the salons of the Cleopatra Club, its owner Calvin Candie (Leonardo DiCaprio) is overseeing a "Mandingo fight" between two strong blacks. The fight does not take place in a ring, but just at one end of a room, surrounded by the chairs of spectators—an absurd, impractical, and unsafe arrangement, given that these men are fighting to the death. (There is no evidence that slave owners ever had such gladiatorial contests, by the way.)

After a lot of grunting and some eye-gouging, Candie orders the victorious slave to dispatch his opponent with a claw hammer. Later Candie orders a runaway slave torn to pieces by dogs. This is a disgustingly sadistic movie: the Marquis de Sade meets *Uncle Tom's Cabin* (a characterization I was saving for *Mandingo* [1975], which now seems like a Jane Austen adaptation by comparison).

The message of this movie to blacks is that white people are loathsome sadists and morons who should be killed with utmost brutality and dispatch. Louis Farrakhan described the movie as "preparation for race war." White people have died because of this movie, just as white people have died because of the lies Anderson Cooper and other media people told about George Zimmerman and Trayvon Martin.

Thus we should count ourselves fortunate that *Django Unchained* is so long and boring (at 2 hours and 45 minutes) that it puts insuperable demands on the average black attention span. (At least we'll know for sure next summer, if babies start turning up with names like Broomhilda and Phrenology.)

If Tarantino had merely wanted to whip up blacks into a murderous rage against whites, he would have made a very different movie. But Tarantino had quite another audience in mind. Tarantino wants an Oscar. He wants it *bad*. Thus *Django Unchained* is another Jewish wet dream. This is a movie calculated to appeal to Jewish hatred of white Americans. Specifically, *Django Unchained* is about the Jewish strategy of using blacks as biological weapons of mass destruction against whites. (Released on Christmas Day, so Jews could see it either before or after dinner at a Chinese restaurant.)

The key to the filmmaker's intent is that Christoph Waltz plays the character of Django's partner, Dr. Schultz, as Jewish.

When Dr. Schultz first appears, he is driving a little peddler's wagon with a large, spring-mounted model of a tooth bobbing drolly on top. He is an itinerant dentist with a foreign accent. He is physically small and nonthreatening, with a shambling gait, his arms and hands held close to his body. He is a real talker though, with a smooth patter and large vocabulary that the stupid, taciturn *goyim* find off-putting.

But appearances are deceptive, because Dr. Schultz is actually a cold, calculating killer who employs complex subterfuges and a gun up his sleeve to get his way. He is a bounty-hunter, who prefers to bring them in dead. He likens his work to the slave trade: human flesh for cold, hard cash. But his wares can't run away.

Hateful fantasies about teaming up with blacks to harm whites are staples of the Jewish imagination. During the 2008 US presidential campaign, Sandra Bernhard warned Sarah Palin to stay away from the Jewish stronghold of New York City lest she be "gang-raped by my big black brothers."[2] During the 2012 US presidential campaign, Bill Maher warned whites not to vote for Mitt Romney because "Black people know who you are, and they will come after you."[3]

But the black-Jewish alliance against whites goes far beyond the fantasies of psychopaths with media megaphones. It is an integral part of the Jewish community's strategy for advancing its collective interests in America.

As Andrew Hamilton ably sums up in "Jews and Slavery: Three Books by the Nation of Islam," before the Civil War, Jews were overrepresented among the people who created and benefited from Negro slavery. Furthermore, they played almost no role in abolishing it.[4]

However, as Kevin MacDonald exhaustively documents in "Jews, Blacks, and Race,"[5] after the immigration of millions of East European Jews at the end of the 19th century, Jews began to regard black civil rights as a way that they could increase their own communal power by eroding the power of the white majority. Thus Jews have taken the lead in promoting black political emancipation, social mobility, and cultural visibility — all at the expense of the white majority.

***

It is, of course, impossible for the director of *Pulp Fiction* to create 2 hours and 45 minutes of film that are completely devoid of charm, although *Django Unchained* is truly Tarantino's worst

---

[2] http://youtu.be/nGhoYT84Jeg

[3] http://youtu.be/Q1-YnorKJsM

[4] http://www.counter-currents.com/2012/08/jews-and-slavery-three-books-by-the-nation-of-islam/

[5] http://www.counter-currents.com/2012/02/jews-blacks-race/

effort. My favorite parts are Fritz the horse, the Spaghetti Western music, and Samuel L. Jackson's performance as Calvin Candie's loathsome and obsequious head house nigger Stephen.

Stephen enjoys great familiarity with and influence over Massa Candie. In front of others, he is the Massa's faithful echo: "Yassa, dass right." But in private he pours himself the Massa's cognac and tells him what's what. Yet he is so jealous of his status as head nigger that he never considers doing anything for the good of his people. Indeed, he is more zealous about degrading his fellow blacks than Candie himself, who is a proven sadist.

Jackson is a brilliant actor. All he needed to bring this role alive was five minutes watching Tarantino interacting with Harvey Weinstein.

Counter-Currents/*North American New Right*,
January 29, 2013

The Matrix Reloaded

About twenty minutes into *The Matrix Reloaded* I was feeling sick to my stomach — literally. The scene was in "Zion," the last bastion of the human [sic] race. Picture the ugliest industrial junkyard on the planet and then drop it down a hole to the ninth circle of hell.

Morpheus, played by the ugly, fat, pockmarked, gap-toothed Negro Laurence Fishburne has just delivered a speech in that deep, resonant, over-modulated, phony-sounding stage voice that Negro actors are wont to use — an affectation that leads me to think that the speaker only half-understands what he is saying.

Then the jungle drums start beating, and we are treated to an excruciatingly long dance/orgy intercut with the lovemaking of Neo (Keanu Reeves) and Trinity (Carrie-Anne Moss, already looking like a crone with a facelift or two). More than 90% of the revelers are non-white: Negroes, Orientals, Mystery Meat. There were even Polynesians with face tattoos. (Or maybe they were just record store clerks from L.A.)

I did not spot any sombreros or bandoliers.

Then, in close succession, I was treated to a spider-strand of spit glistening between the mouths of Trinity and Neo and the slow-motion spectacle of a blue-black, dreadlocked African primitive shaking himself like a wet dog and showering his partners with droplets of sweat. I gagged. My lunch was halfway up my throat before I could control the reflex.

My mind was racing. I was thinking: if this is what the human race is coming to, I would prefer it become extinct. Let the forests grow back. Let the beasts of land, sea, and air multiply. Let them tremble again before worthier kings than man: lions, eagles, great white sharks. (To borrow sentiments from Savitri Devi.)

Then I realized: the human race has *already* come to this. The world is already close to 90% non-white, and since there are no real barriers to non-white immigration, the only thing that stands between us and Zion is . . . time. Zion is the end of our present road of migration and miscegenation. And it is singularly appropriate that this decadent and debased world is called "Zion," because the Jews are primarily responsible for promoting it.

But I would just call it "Hell," and I hope that I was not the only white person in that theater who was nauseated by the spectacle. Honestly, I do not think that most whites are brainwashed and deracinated enough yet to view that scene without some unease. This is the world that is being prepared for you, my brothers and sisters in race: your cultures, your genes, your lives and aspirations, submerged and obliterated in a tide of mud to the mindless, monotonous thumping of jungle drums.

I really wanted to walk out, but I thought of my duty to my readers and resisted the impulse. My mind was swarming with clever titles for negative reviews, but then . . . somehow . . . I started liking this movie.

Yes, the casting is ridiculous: a complete inversion of reality with an anti-white genocidal agenda. Virtually all the villains are white men: big, clean-cut, athletic white men; handsome, sophisticated, French-speaking white men; brilliant, professorial white men. The heroes, however, are a very different, very "diverse" bunch: dreadlocked bucks, high-yellahs with cool shades, patronizing old mammies oozing bullshit from every pore, gooks of the fleet-footed and pencil-necked varieties, all manner of career girls, lipless dykes with spiky hair, Cornel West, and other assorted freaks and misfits. I am surprised that there were no openly Jewish or gay male heroes. I suspect that the Learned Elders of Zion were actually played the Berkeley City Council.

Of course the main hero is Keanu Reeves. Tall and handsome, with almond eyes, high cheekbones, flower petal sunglasses, and a black cassock, he looks like a Slavic priest and flies through the air like Superman. But he is half white, one quarter Chinese, and one quarter Hawaiian, so he doesn't really count either.

Looking at a movie like this, you would almost believe that white civilization could not have been created without the contributions of blacks, browns, yellows, Jews, pathological misfits, stressed-out career twats, etc. In fact, just the opposite is true. Their contributions — if there really are any *net* contributions at all, once you deduct all the destruction caused by such people — are *wholly dispensable*. White civilization could exist without them. But they could not exist without white civilization. These people are parasites. (No, white civilization could not exist without women — wives and mothers — but it could get along very well without career girls. Women's work is the same in every culture. What makes cultures distinct is primarily the work of men.)

Yet Hollywood broadcasts the lie that the parasites are necessary while the hosts are not. This is deadly. It is deadly to everyone, for once the host perishes, so will the parasites. The Jews think that by pushing this poison, they are advancing their collective interests. But they are deluded. They too will be destroyed by the system they are creating. Thus it is tempting to say that the Jews themselves are ultimately just pawns of a larger cosmic force, a force of darkness and evil, death and decay, a force that seeks to arrest and reverse life's upward striving and return the splendid diversity of natural forms that have evolved to the blind chaos of undifferentiated matter, the primordial mud. (Excuse me, I was momentarily possessed by the character of "the Architect.")

But I asked myself: Is there anything about this movie besides the casting that is anti-white? If the same script were shot with a different cast, would there be anything objectionable? The answer is no. *The Matrix Reloaded* is entertaining, thought provoking, and beautifully crafted. And, aside from most of the cast, it is wonderful to look at. It has something for everyone: fantastic fights and car chases for the video game and NASCAR fans, philosophical conundrums, and mythical and literary allusions for coffee house intellectuals. This is a movie that is going to be talked and analyzed and enjoyed to death.

An amusing incident: While the screen was filled with brilliant and heroic Negroes, the audience was filled with Negroes of a very different caliber. They heartily enjoyed it when an obsequious white Stepin Fetchit carried the bags of a dreadlocked

Negro (Neo and Trinity carried their own bags). But when a character known as "the Merovingian" began to discourse on freedom and determinism, I looked around and saw only eyes like pop-up headlights. When the Architect took half a reel to explain how the matrix allows and then co-opts rebellion, they started fidgeting and talking and tittering. Soon a good number of them decided this was a good time for a bafroom break. They must have felt like they were in school or something.

Both *Matrix* movies are useful for White Nationalists. The casting is so blatantly anti-white that it provides an excellent elementary lesson in propaganda.

The Matrix movies also offer a vivid and compelling image of a world precisely analogous to our own: The human race has become enslaved by a race of mechanical parasites (the Jews). The machines keep humanity docile by hiding their slavery from them (ideology). The machines accomplish this by using technology to link human minds together (the mass media) and create an illusory world in which the slaves think that they control their own destinies (consumerism, democracy). This is, of course, a modern version of the parable of the cave in Plato's *Republic*, in which an enslaved humanity is bewitched by a shadow play cast on the cave wall by puppeteers.

As in the parable of the cave, some people break free from this illusory world to live in the real world. They return, however, to the illusory world from time to time, to help free the minds of others who are trapped there. Most people resist them, however, because almost nobody wants to hear that his life—his friends, his family, the ideals he cherishes, the places and things that he loves—are all unreal.

This presents some options that all would-be revolutionaries should contemplate. Do we unplug the matrix and liberate people by destroying their lives? This seems to be the preference of the crazed emancipators of *The Matrix*. Or do we simply leave humanity in chains and enjoy our freedom with a select group of friends in the real world? It might be a kindness to leave people their illusions, but it is not a kindness to leave them their chains. But there is a third, truly humane option: to eliminate the parasites and leave people's cherished illusions intact. This would be accomplished not by unplugging the matrix, but by taking control of it, by placing power not in the hands of parasitic and exploitative foreigners, but in the hands of an elite drawn from the people, an elite with a sense of organic connection to it and responsibility for it.

One thing that I did not like about the first movie is that it seemed metaphysically incoherent. On the one hand, the whole matrix system was perfectly consistent with a non-mystical, scientific naturalism: Plato's cave created by modern science. On the other hand, there was a mystical element: "the Oracle" and the "prophecies" of a savior, "the One." Furthermore, at the end, love conquers death when Trinity brings Neo back to life. Although this movie does not exactly explain how love conquered death in the first movie, Neo returns the favor in a way that follows the rules of the matrix.

I was pleased, however, that *Reloaded* does explain the Oracle and the prophecies in terms of the rules of the matrix. As I understand it, in the world of these movies, freedom is a real and perpetually destabilizing force. Thus the machines needed a way to control it. When the first human rebellion rose against the machines, they crushed it, but appreciated that future rebellions were inevitable. Rebellion cannot be eliminated, but only contained. Therefore, the machines planted the seeds of the next rebellion by starting Zion over again, to serve as a haven for the people who would eventually awake from the matrix. But this time, they sought to control the rebellion by creating the Oracle and her prophecies. After all, what is prophecy? A prophecy is a prediction of the future, and if one believes that one's future has been predicted, then one believes that one does not have any real freedom. Prophecy is, therefore, a way of controlling people's freedom by convincing them that they are not free, but instead are merely realizing a predetermined destiny.

Now, if I have understood this correctly, this seems to be a very good illustration of two important truths. First, the best way for a system to suppress rebellion is not to crush it, but to encourage phony forms of rebellion that safely channel discontent into dead-ends. Second, if the system cannot crush freedom, it will try to denature it by promoting religious superstitions about "destiny," "providence," "oracles," "fate," etc. Doesn't this cast some light on our popular culture?

If you are a White Nationalist and enjoy science fiction and action movies, then I recommend *The Matrix Reloaded* for two reasons. First, if you can manage to keep your lunch down for the first twenty minutes, there is much to enjoy. Second, millions of bright young white people are going to see this movie. They are going to like it, because there are many genuinely likeable things about it. It will make a very strong impression on them; its images and ideas will stick with them, including the image of the hellish mud pits of Zion. Movies like this are the myths and the literature of our post-literate culture. Yes, the movie is a piece of enemy propaganda, but it is clumsy propaganda for their cause and good propaganda for ours. It can easily be seized and turned against them. Just the sort of fancy fighting this movie is famous for.

VNN, May 20, 2003

The Matrix Revolutions

Spoiler: Neo and Trinity die and the machines win. Bummer. Most of the rest makes no sense.

I hated this movie.

I didn't hate it for its racial politics, which are the absolute worst I have ever seen. There are wise, powerful, competent, heroic Negroes everywhere. (The fact that they are all in Zion, a fictional city buried near the center of the Earth, explains why I never encounter them in real life.) There are also so many examples of South-East Asian and Polynesian mystery meat, complete with topknots and facial tattoos, that I scurried home to consult my copy of Carleton Coon's *Living Races of Mankind*, which I like to call the *Field Guide to Featherless Bipeds*.

But as I indicated in my review of *The Matrix Reloaded*, I was willing to overlook the racial politics of the first two *Matrix* films because of their very real virtues.

No, what really offended me about *Revolutions* is the film's sheer god-awful stupidity.

First, there were the continuity problems. Although *Revolutions* is set only hours after *Reloaded*, there are references backward to events that did not happen in the second film. (Or, if they did happen they were so forgettable that, well, I forgot them.) A number of characters also appeared out of nowhere, but acted as if they had already been introduced. The Oracle was played by a different mammy, as the previous mammy had died (without issue, I pray). Allusions were made to the change, but no real explanation was offered. After a while, I began to wonder if this was actually the fourth *Matrix* film or if the projectionist had misplaced a reel or two.

The plot of this movie is also terrible. There is simply no satisfying resolution of the story lines established in the first two films. The final act is no place to introduce new characters who play absolutely no essential role whatsoever (the Indian family in the train station). The final act is no place to bring back old characters for no particular reason (the Merovingian). The final act is no place to give center stage to forgettable non-characters who shouldn't even have been introduced in the second movie (Link, Locke, Niobe, a Negress with the world's biggest lips, the white Stepin Fetchit, Cornel West, etc.).

Pretty much the whole first half of the movie consisted of pointless, wasted scenes with characters I did not care about. It was nothing but fights, chases, and big brown heads looming up to robotically deliver totally uninteresting lines.

One whole sequence seemed to exist only to show the Negress Captain Niobe humiliating a white male captain by showing her superior piloting skills. The fact that on average women are inferior drivers to men because they have inferior visual-spatial skills, and the fact that the average Negro has about half a billion fewer brain cells than the average white and reacts at a much slower rate to stimuli, just go to show that this is science fiction.

And when the Zionists fight off the sentinels, we see slow-reacting blacks and browns manning the guns, while white males see to the reloading.

We are also treated to scenes of two women, one a dyke, attacking sentinel drilling machines with a bazooka. Another good use of superior female visual-spatial skills and upper body strength.

But one subplot particularly grated on me: The idealistic white Stepin Fetchit grovels before and is dressed down by some sort of Mongoloid-Australoid hybrid who is his fearless commander. Later, after taking courage from his commander's dying words, he goes on to complete the mission at great risk of life and limb. He is a role model for whites in the real world created by Zion: we must all get used to taking orders from, fighting for, and dying for our racial inferiors.

Only in the second half of the movie, when the focus was mostly on Neo and Trinity trying to save the day, was my interest piqued. I wish the whole movie had been centered on the surviving core characters from the first film: Neo, Trinity, Morpheus, and Agent Smith. Competent writers could have created such a story. Incompetent writers felt the need to fill the story with new characters and pointless scenes hoping, somehow, to generate interest.

I was appalled by the sheer senselessness of the movie's climax. A central rule of good fiction, especially science fiction, is that the story need not be possible but only plausible. The first *Matrix* movie established a captivatingly plausible world and pretty much stayed within the rules of that world. Ditto for the second movie. But in *Revolutions* the rules established by the first movie are thrown to the wind and nothing is done to make the changes plausible.

The machines have burrowed into Zion, and the Zionists are desperately fighting off great swarms of sentinels. The Zionists fight by strapping themselves into big robots, but for all their formidable technology, these robots provide absolutely no protection for their operators. They do not even have windshields, much less protection from shrapnel and kamikaze sentinels. Stupid Zionists.

The sentinel swarms are visually striking, but I wonder why the machines just didn't pump Zion full of Zyklon B and be done with it? (They couldn't flood it with mud and sewage because, genetically speaking at least, it is already chock-full.)

I guess the answer is provided by the Architect in *Reloaded*, who tells Neo that Zion is needed as a safety valve for the Matrix. Since human freedom cannot be destroyed, the Matrix needs a place to send rebellious types to keep them occupied plotting doomed revolutions.

As Zion is about to fall, Neo pilots a hovercraft to the machine city. This is a visually striking sequence too. The machines try to destroy Neo, but fail. He crashes, and Trinity is killed. Then, once he is completely vulnerable, the machines do not finish him off, but instead decide to talk. Why? No reason is given for their change of policy. It simply makes no sense.

Neo strikes a bargain with the machines. (How does he know they will keep their word? Do machines have a sense of honor?) They will call off their attack on Zion if Neo does them a favor. But doesn't the Architect in *Reloaded* say that Zion will be started again by the machines no matter what, so apparently they were already going to stop the war at some point?

Agent Smith, who began to replicate himself in *Reloaded*

(How? Why?), is beginning to run amok, absorbing other programs and taking over the matrix (How? Why?). The machines can't stop him (Why not?). But Neo can (How?). Agent Smith even manages to take over the minds of people in the real world (How?).

The climactic battle between Neo and Smith is visually exciting, but since the rules of the matrix have been forgotten, the whole thing seems totally arbitrary.

In the midst of the battle, Smith pauses for a moment for his midlife crisis. He asks what it's all about. Why does life go on? Why does Neo continue to fight? It is quite a speech, quite a build-up. We are led to feel that Neo's answer will be highly significant, perhaps the key to the meaning of the whole trilogy. His answer is: "Because I choose to."

It's like watching the titanic labor pains of an elephant, but in the end out pops a mouse.

Neo still defeats Smith. But how? What really happens to Smith? What was Neo's edge? Virtue? Strength? There is no answer, so Smith could just as well have defeated Neo. It makes no sense.

After defeating Smith, Neo apparently dies and is carried off on a hovercraft like Arthur to Avalon. Freed of Smith and Neo, the machines are in the position to finish off Zion completely, but they call off the attack.

The white Stepin Fetchit sees the machines leaving. There could be any number of reasons for this, but having seen the script, he immediately concludes that the war is over and proclaims the news. The mud people begin to gyrate with joy. Zion is saved. We are supposed to feel happy, but nobody in the audience seemed particularly jubilant because by that point the movie had become numbingly uninvolving.

And what about liberating the human race from slavery? Has that been called off? Wouldn't that be a satisfying end to the movie? Wasn't that what the war was all about? Preserving Zion is not a victory over the machines, but part of their policy. So I guess the machines have won.

Meanwhile, back in the Matrix, the Oracle meets the Architect in a park. The Architect promises that some humans will be freed. (Of course some of them will: that is why Zion is necessary.) Then the Oracle looks off into a rainbow-tinted dawn and says that she didn't know that any of it was going to happen, she just "believed." I guess that was the mouse's afterbirth. What a bunch of horseshit.

Don't waste your time with this movie. If you liked *The Matrix* and *The Matrix Reloaded*, *The Matrix Revolutions* can only diminish your enjoyment.

VNN, November 14, 2003

Twilight

Catherine Hardwicke's movie *Twilight* is based on the first novel of a series by Stephenie Meyer. The books mostly appeal to young women, and the advertisements for the movie screamed "chick flick," so I gave it a pass when it was released in theaters. But I admire Joss Whedon's series *Angel*, about a vampire with a soul, and when I heard that *Twilight* centers around a similar character, I was intrigued enough to order it on DVD.

I am glad I did, because *Twilight* is an excellent movie: beautifully filmed, artfully directed, well-acted, with a gorgeous cast and scenery, and very good music. But most importantly, although it is decked out in the usual Semitically-correct Hollywood clichés, the overall message and impression of *Twilight* is quite subversive of Hollywood's agenda. This is particularly interesting since it is directed at young adults, who are the main targets of Hollywood's pro-feminist and anti-white propaganda.

Twilight begins with Bella Swan (played by Kristen Stewart) leaving her mother in sunny Phoenix to finish out her junior year in high school with her father in Forks, Washington. Located on the Olympic Peninsula, Forks is blanketed almost year-round by clouds, fog, and rain.

Bella is a lovely brown-eyed brunette with an exceptionally fair complexion, which gives her a somewhat "Goth" look, although for all I know this analogy is hopelessly dated. Even her name connotes white beauty, for *bella* is Italian for beautiful, and swans are archetypically white and graceful.

Despite her "Goth" look, Bella is not merely a moody and maladjusted teen with morbid tastes. She is a remarkably mature, intelligent, bookish, and sensitive girl who studied ballet and knows something about classical music.

For a small town in Washington State, Forks has an implausible number of non-whites. The only non-whites who really fit in this setting are the local Indians, who are on quite friendly terms with Bella and her father, the local police chief. (Out West in the real world, Indians are overrepresented among criminals and tend not to have warm relations with policemen.)

The students Bella meets are a friendly enough bunch, but they seem immature and one-dimensional compared to her. Bella's attention, however, is immediately drawn to Edward Cullen (played by Robert Pattinson). Tall and handsome, Edward, like Bella, is a brown-eyed brunette with a fair complexion. It looks like makeup, and I am sure the effect is achieved by makeup and lighting, but in close-ups one can see blue veins beneath his skin. Edward's parents Carlisle and Esme (played by Peter Facinelli and Elizabeth Reaser) share Edward's pallor. Strangely, it is also shared by Edward's four foster siblings: Emmet and Rosalie (played by Kellan Lutz and Nikki Reed) and Alice and Jasper (played by Ashley Greene and Jackson Rathbone), who, to add to the weirdness, also seem to be romantic couples.

Edward is obviously as attracted to Bella as she is to him. But he also resists this attraction and flees Bella, which only increases her fascination. She begins to notice strange things about Edward. His eyes change color; his skin is ice cold; he is astonishingly fast and strong; and he and his entire family disappear on the rare days when the sun shines in Forks. . . . You see where this is leading.

The Cullens are vampires. But there is a twist. They do not want to be monsters. Although they have a strong craving for human blood, they resist it and feed on animals instead. As they put it, they are the vampire equivalent of vegetarians. But resisting the hunger is hard, so they are forced to remain aloof from normal people. Edward, however, is in love with Bella. Hence an exquisite conflict: how can he get close enough to love her without succumbing to the temptation to eat her?

I will say no more about the plot of *Twilight*. Suffice it to say that the romance of Edward and Bella is fascinating: emotionally and morally complex, beautifully acted and directed, and just plain hot. But, remarkably, all of this is portrayed without resorting to depictions of nudity and sex.

Aside from the absurdly multi-racial cast of bit-players, the heart of *Twilight* is deeply politically incorrect in three ways.

First, the heroes of *Twilight* are two very unusual teenagers. Edward and Bella are intelligent, thoughtful, well-mannered, serious-minded, and cultured. This is not surprising in the case of Edward, who has lived for more than a century. But Bella really is a teenager. *Twilight* does not mock manners and refined tastes as stuffy, snobbish, and old-fashioned. It displays them in their full beauty and shows that they are consistent with being young, fun-loving, and sexy. This is remarkable message for a movie aimed at a young audience.

The second politically incorrect feature of *Twilight* is the movie's aesthetic of whiteness. One does not need slogans like "White is Beautiful," because it is so obvious. But while the cultural establishment exploits the white racial aesthetic, it also undermines it, particularly by promoting the ideas that tanning is beautiful and healthy-looking while having a fair complexion is ugly and unhealthy looking. (Of course a corpse-like pallor does look unhealthy, but a fair complexion that is rosy and pink with health obviously does not. Tanning, as Socrates pointed out, does not make people healthy; it merely adds color to the sick and the healthy alike, allowing one to mask one's sickliness.) Promoting tanning is the cosmetic equivalent of miscegenation: it replaces distinctly white characteristics with non-white ones. (One can, of course, lose one's tan, but not the skin damage that comes with it. Miscegenation, however, is forever.)

Bella and the Cullens are, of course, a whiter shade of pale. Too white to really be healthy. But nonetheless, they force you to confront just how beautiful palefaces can be. They look like they have stepped out of old paintings from the days when people valued fair complexions and tried to preserve them. Of course all the actors have fine features, which is the bedrock of beauty no matter what the skin tone. But their fair skin, especially combined with dark hair and eyes and red lips, makes their faces astonishingly expressive in the most subtle ways. (*Twilight* promotes a white aesthetic, but not a blonde-haired, blue-eyed one, since these contrast less strikingly with fair skin.) Facial expressiveness is a matter of contrasts, and the fairer the complexion, the wider the range of contrasts that can be observed, from the most subtle blush to the most marked expressions of fear and anger. (This, by the way, is why blacks rely so heavily on their eyes and teeth to express their emotions, since these contrast most sharply with their complexions.)

The third way in which *Twilight* is politically incorrect is that the whole thrust of the movie is deeply anti-feminist. In one scene, Bella tells one of her racially indeterminate schoolmates that she should ask a guy to the prom rather than wait for him to ask her, because she is "a strong, independent woman." This strong, independent woman takes Bella's advice and gets the date she wants: a flamboyantly effeminate Chinese wimp. Together, they are the feminist establishment's ideal androgynous couple, and nobody in his or her right mind would want to emulate them.

Bella, however, is not interested in the nice, non-threatening boys in her high school. She only has eyes for Edward, because she senses that he has powerful emotions that he is struggling to keep in check. She is attracted to him because he is dangerous. But even when she unravels Edward's secret, she is not dissuaded from pursuing him, but instead is even more fascinated.

There is a remarkable exchange between Bella and Edward once they openly acknowledge that he is a vampire. He says that she should flee from him. He is the most dangerous predator in nature. Everything about him is designed to attract her: his looks, his voice, his smell. But if she tried to run away from him, he could outrun her. If she tried to fight him off, he could overpower her. It is only the strength of his will and chivalrous instincts, and his desire for a deeper and longer-lasting form of union, that protects her.

Bella is no *Buffy the Vampire Slayer*, no *Xena: Warrior Princess*. Edward makes her feel anything but strong and independent. That is what makes him so irresistible. But he does make her feel deeply feminine, and deeply powerful in a different way. For Edward, despite all of his strength, is incomplete, and as a woman Bella possesses something that has made this fierce and formidable killer helplessly in love with her. Yet loving her does not emasculate him, and this is good, because the same strength and capacity for violence that could be used to rape or kill her allows Edward to go on to save Bella from being raped and killed by others.

Edward's potential for violence and the chivalry that holds it in check may be heightened by his vampire nature, but there is nothing supernatural about them. Edward Cullen is what in decades past was known as a red-blooded American male. Bella too is a classic figure from fiction: a damsel whose awareness of her physical weakness and vulnerability only heightens her sense of a woman's true strength.

Of course for decades now the popular culture has worked to emasculate men and masculinize women: to turn men into the non-threatening males Bella spurns and to convince women that strength lies in casting aside all distinctly female roles and competing with men in traditionally male pursuits (or driving their men crazy in trying).

It is a testimony to the power of this propaganda that true manliness can now appear only in the guise of a monster. It is a testament to the even greater power of nature that women find the monster irresistible nonetheless.

TOQ Online, May 2, 2009

Twilight: New Moon

The news is: the movie of *New Moon*, the second installment of Stephenie Meyer's *Twilight Saga*, doesn't suck—in the vulgar, colloquial, non-vampire sense of the word—although all the signs were certainly there.

First, the book of *New Moon* is terrible: nearly 600 pages of pedestrian prose, glacially paced, padded to excruciating lengths not with fluff, but with damp, insipid, indigestible literary sawdust. (Don't any of the big publishers employ decent editors? I am not asking for Victor Hugo every time I pick up a work of popular fiction, but could we at least have Stephen King?) Worst of all, the most compelling character, Edward Cullen was absent throughout much of the book. The only thing that got me to pick the book back up after flinging it down several times in dismay was the hope that finally the romance of Bella Swan and her vampire lover Edward Cullen would resume.

Second, Catherine Hardwicke, the superb director of the first *Twilight* movie, was replaced by Chris Weitz, and the previews of the movie were not promising. Frankly, they are as flat and dull as the novel.

But I have to hand it to Weitz and scriptwriter Melissa Rosenberg: they managed to extract a compelling two hour movie from the sprawling mess of the novel. *New Moon* is not as good as *Twilight*, but it is a worthy successor and a bridge to the final two novels/films, which promise much more. The momentum has not been lost.

Part of what makes *New Moon* work is simply the lingering magic of the first film. We were all glad to see the familiar characters and settings again.

Beyond that, Weitz manages to condense vast boring tracts of the novel into tightly paced, compelling scenes, many of them wordless. The literary sawdust has been replaced with visual poetry—and light comedy.

But the best thing about *New Moon* is the performance of Taylor Lautner as Jacob Black. Although in the book, Jacob seems merely a distraction and digression from the main plot, Taylor Lautner's performance made this movie his own. Amazingly, when he was on the screen, we did not miss Edward Cullen. Lautner is a fine, sensitive actor, with a magnificent physique, imposing stage presence, and genuine animal magnetism (which comes in handy for playing a werewolf).

(Guys: I saw this movie with an audience that was 90 percent white, 80 percent under 30, and 80 percent female, and I can tell you if you don't already know: women go for muscles. They might *say* something different, but their gasps, sighs, and flutters told a whole different story.)

My two main criticisms of this movie are that the computer animated werewolves look fake, and the Cullens mostly look terrible. In the first film, they are lighted and made up to seem pale but beautiful and strong, like marble statues. In *New Moon*, they look like corpses who have just awakened from a decades-long nap, with the bad hair one would expect.

Now, as a white racialist, what is my take on this movie? In my review of *Twilight*, I emphasized that I liked three aspects of that movie.

First, even though the movie added in a number of non-white bit characters, it largely follows the book in underscoring the beauty of white people. *New Moon* undermines this, by making the Cullens look unappealing and by placing the spotlight on Jacob Black and his fellow young American Indians, who are portrayed by exceptionally handsome, muscular, and fit actors. By the way, judging from the biographies of the actors as well as their looks, all of them seem to have some white ancestry, despite their coppery complexions, which gives them longer, handsomer faces rather than typically round, ugly Amerindian faces.

Although there is a deep friendship—and the seeds of romance—between Jacob and Bella, in the end she returns to Edward. However, the movie can only promote miscegenation through its portrayal of an unusually handsome and gallant non-white male. White girls considering such dalliances in the real world need to realize that race-mixing destroys all races that take part in it. They also need to look at statistics on non-white tendencies towards infecting white women with STDs, raping them, and abandoning, abusing, and murdering them and their children.

Second, I liked how *Twilight* portrayed Bella Swan and Edward Cullen as exceptionally mature, cultured, and well-mannered young people—without implying that these qualities in any way detract from them being fun-loving and sexy. *New Moon* does nothing to undermine this, but it does nothing to add to it either.

Third, *Twilight* emphasizes traditional sex roles. Edward Cullen and Jacob Black are not today's silly, weak, effeminate, non-threatening males. They are strong, masculine, gallant, heroic, and a little dangerous. Bella Swan is no ass-kicking *Buffy the Vampire Slayer*. She is physically weaker than Edward and Jacob and attracted to their strength—including the dangers that come with it—and grateful for their protection. (Bella requires a lot of rescuing.) *New Moon* reinforces this aspect of the story, with Jacob and his wolf pack taking on the role of rescuers.

Yet Bella is in full possession of her real strength as a woman, which makes both men willing to sacrifice themselves to protect her. They do not want to live without her, but they both break off their relationships with her, because they fear that their supernatural strength threatens her well-being. Both come to learn, however, that Bella is safer with them than without them.

When Edward thinks that Bella is dead and seeks to end his life, Bella takes on the role of the rescuer, appearing in the nick of time to save his life, not through strength, but simply because she is the one who makes his life complete.

Echoing my review of *Twilight*: in spite of their supernatural powers, Edward Cullen and Jacob Black are what in decades past were known simply as red-blooded males. Because of the sickness of our society, such men today can appear on the screen only in the guise of monsters. But because of the strength of nature, women find the monsters irresistible nonetheless.

White people should see *New Moon*, but the parents of young girls need to warn them about the consequences of miscegenation in the real world.

TOQ Online, November 20, 2009

Twilight: Eclipse

Twilight: Eclipse is the third movie based on Stephenie Meyer's phenomenally popular four-volume *Twilight Saga*.

First, some background.

In *Twilight*, Bella Swan (Kristin Stewart), the protagonist with whom millions of primarily white teenage girls identify, comes to live with her father in Forks, Washington, one of the rainiest places in the United States. She is a junior in high school. There she meets the handsome and mysterious Edward Cullen (Robert Pattinson), who turns out to be a vampire.

Edward is in love with Bella, but it requires all of his superhuman strength and old-fashioned chivalry to restrain his desire to eat her. Bella loves Edward as well, and she is undeterred by his strength and dangerousness. Truth be told, it is part of his attraction. After some harrowing adventures, in which Edward saves Bella's life, Bella asks Edward to make her a vampire too, so they can be together forever.

In the second movie, *New Moon*, a love triangle develops. Edward leaves Bella because he does not wish to make her a vampire and wishes to protect her from the inevitable dangers of associating with his kind. Heartbroken, Bella begins spending time with Jacob Black, an American Indian from the vicinity whom she knew from childhood. Jacob begins to fall in love with Bella, but she can think only of Edward. Oh, and Jacob turns out to be a werewolf. After some harrowing adventures, in which Bella saves Edward's life, the two are reunited. Edward says he will grant Bella's request to become a vampire, but on one condition: that she marry him.

In the third movie, *Eclipse*, the rivalry between Jacob and Edward is turned into a partnership as more harrowing adventures unfold, Jacob withdraws from pursuing Bella, and Bella accepts Edward's proposal of marriage. That's all I'll say about the plot.

It is not hard to explain the popularity of these novels. The premise is imaginative and the stories are well-constructed.

Unfortunately, the novels are executed in an excruciatingly padded and pedestrian manner, so it is best to just see the movies.

What is remarkable about *The Twilight Saga* is just how downright traditional and conservative it is. Advocates of feminism and sexual liberation hate it, and for good reason.

In my earlier reviews, I stated that I liked the *Twilight* movies for three reasons.

1. Edward and Bella are remarkably mature, cultured, articulate, and well-mannered teenagers. Edward, of course, has been a teenager for a very long time. But Bella has not. *The Twilight Saga* teaches young people that being well-mannered and well-spoken and developing a taste for European high culture, is not incompatible with being young, attractive, and fun.

2. The *Twilight* movies promote the aesthetic appreciation of whiteness, since both Bella and the vampires have very pale complexions, which heighten our awareness of the beauty and expressiveness of white features. This effect was strongest in the first *Twilight* movie directed by Catherine Hardwicke. The second movie, directed by Chris Weitz, and the present film, directed by David Slade, somewhat undermine this effect by giving the vampires a creepy, corpse-like pallor.

3. Most importantly, the *Twilight* movies are anti-feminist, emphasizing traditional male and female roles. They are a return to an older form of literature combining chivalry and Gothic horror.

Edward Cullen and Jacob Black are not the silly, non-threatening, emasculated boys of contemporary fiction. They are powerful and dangerous. This power allows them to protect Bella from others, and their chivalry protects her from them.

Bella is not a "strong woman" in the ass-kicking, ball-busting feminist sense. She is fragile, uncoordinated, and frequently in need of rescuing. But she is strong in ways that feminists know nothing about: men will live and die and kill for her, simply because they love her and cannot live without her. When she saves Edward's life in *New Moon*, it is not by feats of strength. It is simply by showing him that she—the one he can't live without—is still alive.

Eclipse, however, revealed to me a whole new traditional dimension of the *Twilight* books, for the core of this movie is a defense of marriage and a critique of premarital sex. Bella echoes the popular culture's attitudes against marriage, particularly against getting married young. But Edward patiently overturns these objections one by one. Moreover, I now see that in the first two books, Bella's desire to become a vampire functions symbolically as a desire for her first sexual experience, and Edward's initial refusal, and then his consent on the condition of marriage, is a rejection of premarital sex and defense of virginity.

In *Eclipse*, this all becomes quite explicit. When Bella's Baby Boomer father tells her that he hopes that she and Edward are using birth control, her flustered and indignant reply is that she is a virgin. Clearly, she wishes that it went without saying. Kids today! Elsewhere in the movie, Bella and Edward are making out, and she tries to push it toward actual sex. He refuses. He wants to get married first.

Now, the very existence of books like *The Twilight Saga* is probably not remarkable. After all, there is a whole genre of Amish romance novels. What is remarkable is that they are immensely popular—so popular that Hollywood wants to make a few hundred million bucks off of them—and so popular that Hollywood dare not tamper with the basic message, no matter how it must grate against the reigning sensibilities in the film industry. (The only politically correct touches come in the casting of non-whites in minor roles that were written as white in the novels.)

There are two other small but important touches of political incorrectness in *Eclipse*. First, the vampire Rosalie speaks of the main disadvantage of being a vampire. Yes, she will be young and beautiful forever. But she will never have the pleasure of seeing her children and grandchildren growing up around her. It is not enough to praise virginity and marriage without making it clear that Bella's inability to experience motherhood is simply tragic. Fortunately, it is a tragedy that the millions of young women who read these books and see these movies need not suffer. Second, the vampire Jasper reveals that before he became a vampire, he was an officer in the Confederate Army. For romance and chivalry, the Union just doesn't cut it!

In my earlier reviews, I remarked that Edward Cullen and Jacob Black are what in the past were simply known as "men." The fact that real men cannot show up in movies except as monsters is a measure of how far our civilization has strayed from nature. But the fact that women find these monsters so attractive shows that nature is stronger in the end. As far as I knew, however, this rejection of feminism was merely implicit.

Eclipse, however, reveals something even more unusual. *The Twilight Saga* is an *explicit* defense of virginity followed by marriage and motherhood and an *explicit* rejection of premarital sex and sexual promiscuity. These themes may be subtle in *Twilight*, but they become more explicit in *New Moon* and quite overt in *Eclipse*.

Thus *The Twilight Saga* is truly something remarkable: an across the board revolt against modern sexual mores in favor of tradition. A revolt by the younger generation against their permissive and degenerate parents in favor of tradition and against what passes today for freedom. (It came as no surprise when I learned that author Stephenie Meyer is a Mormon.)

From a racialist point of view, my only quarrel with *The Twilight Saga* is Bella's relationship with the American Indian Jacob Black. But in the end Bella chooses a man of her own race. My initial instinct would have been to leave out the whole interracial romance, but have changed my mind. Young women today are being bombarded with pro-miscegenation propaganda, so perhaps it is healthier to acknowledge that such temptations exist but show Bella choosing her own kind in the end. (By the way, Taylor Lautner, who played Jacob Black, delivers another smolderingly charismatic performance. He has what it takes to be a major star.)

I highly recommend *Eclipse*. Nobody who enjoyed the first two *Twilight* movies will want to miss it.

Counter-Currents/*North American New Right*,
July 23, 2010

Breaking Dawn, Part 1

Twilight: Breaking Dawn, Part 1, is the fourth and penultimate movie of *The Twilight Saga*, based on Stephenie Meyer's phenomenally popular series of novels. Worldwide, the *Twilight* novels have now sold more than 100 million copies; they have been translated into 37 languages; *The Twilight Saga* movies have grossed more than $2 billion.

Meyer, I am sorry to say, is a terrible writer who nevertheless conceived a rather original and well-plotted take on the vampire and werewolf genres. Meyer, a Mormon mother of three, has also managed a masterstroke of conservative subversion of Leftist cultural hegemony by packaging an essentially traditional (and biological) outlook on male and female psychology, sex, chastity, marriage, and now pregnancy, abortion, and childbirth in the form of Gothic horror novels and tricking the publishing industry and now Hollywood into marketing this message to millions of young and overwhelmingly white females.

The *Twilight* code is basically simple. Traditional sexual morals (which are rooted in biology) have been thoroughly corrupted by feminism and allied anti-natural attitudes, as well as the easy availability of birth control and abortion. But, as Horace observed, you may drive nature out with a pitchfork, but she will find her way back. In this case, nature has returned in the guise of the supernatural.

By nature, males are stronger on average than females. Modern society seeks equality by psychologically feminizing men and masculinizing women. In the first two *Twilight* novels/movies, *Twilight* and *New Moon*, the heroine Bella Swan (Kristen Stewart) thinks of herself as a strong, independent woman. And by comparison to the emasculated boys in her high school, that is true. But none of these boys particularly appeal to her, either.

Then she meets Edward Cullen (Robert Pattinson). There is something different about Edward. It turns out that he is a vampire. He is immensely fast and strong; he can read everybody's mind except Bella's (her inscrutability is a source of attraction);

and he has an overpowering desire to drink her blood, which he resists because he is in love with her. She is willing to take the risk, because she is in love with him. Bella also develops a close friendship with Jacob Black (Taylor Lautner), an American Indian from the nearby reservation. It turns out that Jacob is a werewolf.

So Bella has a thing for bad boys. She is attracted to strong bodies and strong desires and the dangers that come with them — and the noble virtues that keep them in check. Jealousy is also a danger: Jacob is in love with Bella and wants to win her for himself.

Both Edward and Jacob are afraid that their strength will hurt Bella, so both of them break off their relationships with her in order to protect her. But the lesson of the first two movies is that male strength is not a bad thing, for the very strength that could hurt Bella is necessary to save her from harm.

The subversive message to young men doped up on Ritalin and bombarded with emasculating messages is that manliness is a good thing: women are attracted to primal strength and aggression. They want a gentleman with a bit of Neanderthal. And if good men suppress these traits out of the chivalrous desire to avoid any possibility of hurting the women they love, they will lose their women to bad men with no such scruples and repressions. Beneath the monster makeup, Edward and Jacob turn out to be what healthier generations knew merely as "men." So let's hope more young women drag their boyfriends to these "chick flicks" until the message sinks in.

In the third movie, *Eclipse*, another dimension of traditional/biological sexual mores is explored quite explicitly. Traditional ideas about the value of female modesty, chastity, fidelity, and virginity have a basis in biology, namely in the unequal consequences of sex for men and women. For men, the sole consequence of sex (omitting STDs) is a brief but intense pleasure. For women, sex can lead to nine months of pregnancy, with its attendant dangers, followed by years of caring for a child.

Because of these consequences, women needed to be choosy about their sexual partners (hence the values of modesty and virginity). They needed to find men who would be willing to stick around and protect and provide for them and their offspring. And to find such men, they needed to offer reasonable assurances of paternity (hence the value of fidelity).

All of these values have, of course, been undermined at their root by birth control and abortion as well as feminism and general culture of hedonism.

The Twilight Saga provides a new mythical foundation for these virtues by restoring the danger of sex. Bella could just "hook up" with any of the normal guys in her high school. Her father simply advises her to use birth control. But she can't make love so casually to Edward. With his immense strength he might simply crush the life out of her if he gets carried away. (Note to guys: this is a thought that, apparently, titillates millions of young women.)

Bella's solution to the problem of her physical vulnerability (the girl is constantly being menaced by other vampires) is to ask Edward to turn her into a vampire too. This is not merely a metaphor for losing her virginity. It is a practical necessity of doing so. At the end of the second movie, he tells her that he will do so under one condition: that she marry him.

Bella has a head full of modern ideas scorning marriage (she is an only child of divorced parents), especially marrying right out of high school, which of course gets in the way of lots of "partying" and "fun," not to mention the "fulfillment" of college and a career. But Edward will have none of it. He is old-fashioned. (He has been 17 for a very long time.) In an amusing role reversal, it is the man who insists that the woman save her virginity for marriage (just as in the earlier films, it is the woman who teaches the men the value of their strength). At the end of the third film, Bella accepts.

In healthy societies, marriage is a momentous decision. It is a lifetime commitment. Traditional marriage, moreover, is more than the joining of two individuals; it is the joining of two families. This was especially the case when extended families lived under the same roof (as the Cullens do). Thus it is natural that the whole family get involved with a member's decision to marry. They all have a strong stake in the outcome. In more dangerous times, family solidarity can often mean the difference between life and death.

The seriousness of marriage has been destroyed by easy divorce, family breakdown, psychological and social atomization, the welfare state, and the punitive child support system. But all of those concerns come back when you are a clan of vampires contemplating taking a human into your midst.

Edward Cullen's family takes a strong interest in Bella from the very beginning. They want to be absolutely sure that she is right for Edward. My first instinct was that they were prying, and he should tell them all to shove it. But that was just another bit of modernity that I had not managed to purge from my thinking. (It looks like it will take a lifetime.) But the Cullens are right to be concerned with maintaining the solidarity of their clan, and Bella learns that she would not want it any other way, for the world they live in is dangerous, and the whole family needs to be united to survive. Although the Cullens live in a huge modern mansion, in the end, it is really just another log cabin in the American woods where settlers hold off marauding Indians (and werewolves).

Breaking Dawn, Part 1, begins with Edward and Bella's wedding. At this point, I will say a bit more about the film than can be gathered from the trailers, so consider yourself warned. Edward and Bella go to Brazil on their honeymoon. Edward does not transform her into a vampire, because she does not want to spend her honeymoon writhing in pain. She also convinces him to make love to her. In spite of the dangers, he gives in. The next morning, the bedroom looks like the Tasmanian Devil has blown through. But Bella is quite content. She has just a few bruises. Edward is totally contrite, and Bella has to teach him again that she loves him, including his strength, *even if it hurts her*.

Vampires, apparently, cannot have babies. But that is something that Bella was willing to give up to spend an eternity with Edward. To everyone's surprise, however, vampires can *make* babies. Bella finds herself pregnant. Then the movie takes a *Rosemary's Baby* turn. The baby grows at a phenomenal rate, draining Bella's life, cracking her ribs with its super-strong kicks. Edward wants his father, Carlyle (a doctor) to get "that thing" out of her. It is a dangerous pregnancy in a world where medical science has virtually eliminated such dangers. But Bella refuses. It is a "baby," not a "fetus," not a "thing." And she is going to carry it to term, no matter what.

Most people think abortion is immoral, but they can accept it in circumstances when the mother's life is at stake. Feminists, however, regard abortion as a virtual sacrament, and in the case where the life of the mother is threatened, they are not pro-"choice"; they are pro-abortion. Now I ask: where else in this culture, dominated by feminism and the imperative of white race-replacement, are millions of young white women going to be exposed to the example of a young white mother who refuses an abortion because she decides she is willing to risk her life bringing a new child into the world?

I will say no more about the plot, save that it gets quite brutally *intense* near the end—really too intense for kids.

Breaking Dawn, Part 1, is a beautifully filmed movie, with a generally languid pace like the first *Twilight* movie. I liked the pace, but I imagine it might be disconcerting to people raised on MTV and its successors. (There isn't even a music video break, like *Twilight*'s immortal vampire baseball scene.) There is a great deal of gentle humor. The wedding and honeymoon are bridal magazine porn of the highest order. (Although interracial couples were fore-grounded in a scene in Brazil. See my review of *Eclipse* for my take on the Jacob Black question.) The digital werewolves look as fake as ever. (More imaginative filmmakers could have made analog werewolves work much better.) There are some annoying "transformation" special effects.

But there are also moments of pure poetry: when a young man falls to his knees in awe, and when a mother, father, and newborn baby wave to the camera. Honest to God, I blinked back a couple of tears. This is not the best *Twilight* movie, but it is definitely worth seeing.

Counter-Currents/*North American New Right*
November 24, 2011

Breaking Dawn, Part 2

Breaking Dawn, Part 2 is the fifth and final movie of Mormon novelist Stephenie Meyer's phenomenally popular *Twilight Saga*. I think that the *Twilight Saga* is highly significant, because it offers a systematic argument for traditional—and biological—sexual roles and morality in the form of a Gothic teen romance story involving vampires and werewolves.

Breaking Dawn, Part 2, however, is a major disappointment. The movie does not betray or ruin the series, mind you. It is just largely empty and unnecessary. Nor does it contain any positive, traditional messages. It is mostly just an action movie.

I read the first *Twilight* novel to see if the film version had replaced white characters with non-white ones, and it did. I also learned that, while Stephenie Meyer is a genius at cultural subversion and quite clever at constructing characters and plots, she is an excruciatingly bad writer. The bones of her well-constructed plots are padded with layers of literary lard and cellulite—smothering seas of jiggling, gelatinous, blowsy, bloated, swollen, soggy, premenstrual prose. And the second novel, *New Moon*, was even worse, so I never read beyond it.

Meyer's novels made me appreciate the talents of screenwriter Melissa Rosenberg at flensing and rendering these blubbery books down to lean, sinewy scripts. But when the first three movie made more than two billion dollars, the producers hefted *Breaking Dawn*, the fattest of the four novels by far, and—cha-ching!—decided to make two movies out of it, which entailed leaving in a lot of flab. Frankly, if greed had not won out, this story could have been told in a single, two hour movie, and practically everything in the second film could have been left out.

In *Part 1*, Bella Swan marries her vampire love Edward Cullen. Edward insists that he will make her a vampire only after their wedding. But before her transformation, Bella becomes pregnant, which comes as a shock, because nobody knew it was possible for a vampire to sire a child. The pregnancy endangers Bella's life, but she refuses to have an abortion. Once the baby is born, Edward transforms Bella into a vampire to prevent her from dying from childbirth.

In *Part 2*, Bella and Edward deal with telling Bella's family and the undead community about their special child, before they settle down for eternal happiness. A lot of the story is surprisingly lame, and the rest could have been told in 20 minutes. Much of the movie is devoted to preparing for a battle of the Cullens and their allies (the local werewolves and vampires from around the globe) against the Volturi, their Italian-based elder kindred. This battle is based on a mistake and never even happens in the end (a giant emotional cheat and failure of moral nerve). But it involves the introduction of a vast cast of forgettable paper-thin bit characters (many of them non-white) only to dismiss them later.

Part 2 also contains some distasteful race-mixing. Sure, Bella had a thing for Jacob Black, a local American Indian, but she ended up with a man of her own race. Now Bella's dad has taken up with a local squaw, and it is suggested that Jacob may end up with Bella's daughter.

Just as *Star Wars* fans have effectively excised *The Phantom Menace* from the canon,[1] I suggest dropping *Breaking Dawn, Part 2*. If you haven't seen it yet, just pretend that the *Twilight Saga* ends with *Breaking Dawn, Part 1*.

Counter-Currents/*North American New Right*
November 28, 2012

---

[1] http://www.nomachetejuggling.com/2011/11/11/the-star-wars-saga-suggested-viewing-order/

The Girl with the Dragon Tattoo

For several years now, Stieg Larsson's *The Girl with the Dragon Tattoo* and its two sequels have been among the world's best-selling works of fiction. Of course, I have no time or taste for contemporary popular fiction, so it completely escaped me.

Around last Christmas, however, a friend mentioned the movie version in the context of a conversation about travel in Scandinavia. (The movie was produced and shot in Sweden.) By chance, shortly after that, Netflix included it in a list of movies I might like. On a whim, I added it to my queue, then forgot about it until it showed up in my mailbox a month later.

All of this, of course, is a necessary alibi, because this movie is so stupid, so politically correct, and so downright evil that I never would have watched it if I had known anything about it, aside from where it was filmed.

Stieg Larsson (1954–2004) was a Swedish Communist journalist and activist. He was also a fervent feminist. In his work, he portrays Sweden as a society rife with violence and sadism against women. No, he is not writing about the violence committed by the Muslim and black immigrants that Communists like himself have been inflicting upon Sweden. He is writing about Swedish men.

Now the Vikings did their share of roving and raping and pillaging a millennium ago. I have the blue eyes to prove it. But today, Nordic men are among the most peaceable and law-abiding in the world, and by all objective measures, Nordic women are some of the best off women in the world, although they are now being subjected to increased levels of rape and sexual exploitation by non-white immigrants. (In Stieg Larsson's world, the only immigrants are women, who are raped and murdered by sadistic Swedes.)

But it gets worse. Sweden is, of course, one of Europe's most Left-wing countries. Stieg Larsson's Sweden, however, is menaced by powerful Nazis. That's right. Nazis. Larsson himself claimed that his life was constantly threatened by powerful

Nazis. He refused to marry his long-time girlfriend, telling her, "Sorry baby, if we get hitched, the Nazis might get you too." A gallant defender of women to the end, that Stieg Larsson.

(Larsson's books were published after his death, and under Swedish law, his mistress gets nothing. He wanted his estate to go to the Communist Party, but his will was legally invalid, so all of his royalties go to his father and brother. Surely they could not be worse recipients of a vast fortune than Stieg, his mistress, or the Communist Party.)

These Nazis are, moreover, some of Sweden's leading industrialists. And there's more. One of these families of Nazi industrialists, the Vangers, is about the worst clan since Sawney Beane. There is incest, parricide, and a father-son team of serial rapists and murderers.

To make matters worse, the father, Gottfried Vanger, seems to be a Christian religious enthusiast (in about the least religious country in Europe).

But what is truly unforgivable is his anti-Semitism. His victims are Jews. Including a Jewish farm wife. (Perhaps her family fled Hans Landa's World War II roundup of Jewish dairy farmers in France depicted in *Inglourious Basterds*.) When the Jewish angle is revealed, the good guys—already hip deep in death—react with a special horror that reveals that their deepest sympathies lie with Jews. The whole atmosphere of the movie darkens. Now, the audience is to understand, this evil is really *serious*.

Thus Stieg Larsson is mentally indistinguishable from a Jew in regarding Jewish lives as more valuable than non-Jewish lives, including, presumably, his own. Normal people reserve their deepest horror for the deaths of the people who are closest to them. It is more horrible to lose a friend or family member than a stranger, more horrible to lose a countryman than a foreigner.

But Larsson's characters—who are merely projections of his character—are horrified when they discover that the victims are not their fellow Swedes, but Jews. In Guillaume Faye's terms, they are textbook ethnomasochists and xenophiles. They would prefer their own people to be murdered rather than

Jews (Jews above all) and assorted totemic "others." Sick, sick people.

Gottfried, the sick bastard, teaches his son Martin to be a rapist and serial killer too. The son, however, is rather pleased that he has grown beyond his father's racial and religious views. Martin is modern. He is emancipated from prejudice. He just kills for pleasure.

Sweden did have some prominent Nazis, including the great explorer Sven Hedin (who was part Jewish, but that did not prevent him from befriending Hitler, Goebbels, Göring, and other top Nazis). As a young man, Ingmar Bergman, Sweden's greatest filmmaker was an enthusiastic admirer of Hitler. Ingvar Kamprad, the founder of IKEA and one of the world's richest men, was a follower of Swedish fascist Per Engdahl (who was not a Nazi but a follower of Mussolini). Sweden also has younger generations of neo-Nazis, but they are few, marginalized, powerless, and far less prone to violence than non-white immigrants or Left-wing anti-fascists.

The "good guys" in this movie are the "girl with the dragon tattoo" herself Lisbeth Salander (played by Noomi Norén, who is half Swedish and half Spanish-Gypsy) and Mikael Bomkvist (played by Michael Nyqvist), a Left-wing journalist and defender of women clearly modeled on Larsson himself.

Lisbeth is an emotionally damaged woman who has been mentally hospitalized. She has mutilated her body with multiple piercings and extensive tattoos. Her hair is bottle black. (Even without the ink and hardware, her body is repulsively lean, muscular, and titless.) She works as a hacker: a criminal who snoops in people's private data. She has Asperger's syndrome and has a hard time maintaining personal relationships. She is a lesbian. Oh, and when she was 12 years old, she set her father on fire.

Larsson had the face to claim that Lisbeth is Pippi Longstocking all grown up, which is a pretty good description of the agenda of every Leftist defender of women. Pippi Longstocking was a cute, adventurous little girl with superhuman strength who was the subject of a highly popular series of wholesome Swedish children's books and movies. The feminist idea of progress apparently means turning every bright, spunky, adventurous Pippi Longstocking into a hard, cold, emotionally repressed, alienated, criminal, tattooed, lesbian freak with a face full of hardware.

Of course the modern publishing industry turns out this kind of repulsive, politically correct swill all the time. The reason that Larssen's books are so popular is that—if the movie is any indication—he is actually a good storyteller. The movie is also a very well-made, directed by the Dane Niels Arden Oplev, with a uniformly excellent cast. The character of Martin Vanger is genuinely terrifying in ways never approached by more flamboyant serial killers like Hannibal Lecter.

But it is impossible to recommend such a relentlessly dishonest and stupidly P.C. movie. At least abominations like *The Matrix Reloaded*, *Inglourious Basterds*, and *Machete* can be turned to our advantage with a clever review. But this movie has nothing positive to offer.

The Girl with the Dragon Tattoo is long gone from the theaters. But you have not dodged the bullet yet. Hollywood could not pass up a steaming pile of anti-Nazi, anti-white, pro-feminist propaganda like this. So Jewish director David Fincher (*Fight Club*) is working on an English-language version starring Daniel Craig as Mikael Blomkvist. They are aiming for a December 2011 release. Happy Hanukah!

Counter-Currents/*North American New Right*,
February 10, 2011

The Girl with the Dragon Tattoo
Remake

David Fincher's big-star, big-budget, English-language remake of the 2009 Swedish film *The Girl with the Dragon Tattoo* was certainly not necessary from an artistic point of view. The original film, directed by the Danish director Niels Arden Oplev, was extremely well-acted and well-made. For fans of the novel, it is iconic.

The obvious motive for the remake, of course, was money. Swedish Communist Stieg Larsson's novel and its two sequels are among the world's best-selling novels, but English-speakers, Americans in particular, just don't go for subtitled foreign films.

But is the new film an improvement on the old? Not unless you consider magnifying the original's most distasteful elements to be an improvement. Personally, I found the Swedish version's depictions of violence and sadism repulsive enough.

Fincher is a talented director, with first-rate cinematographers, but in the end, this just comes off as a copy of Oplev's original. It has no life of its own. Fincher assembled a lot of big name actors, but none of them overshadow the performances in the first film. Furthermore, in the remake, Stellan Skarsgård is far less chilling as serial killer Martin Vanger than Peter Haber in the Swedish version.

The only real improvement is the music. Frankly, the original movie's score made no impression on me. Not so with the Trent Reznor/Atticus Ross soundtrack for the remake, particularly the riveting version of Led Zeppelin's "The Immigrant Song" played under the Maurice Binder-like opening credit sequence.

But in addition to the billions Hollywood hopes to rake in from Stieg Larsson's trilogy, they are also counting on a tremendous propaganda boon, for *The Girl with the Dragon Tattoo* is one of most evil, stupid, politically correct, and anti-white books ever written—so evil, in fact, that it must have stung some egos in Hollywood that a Swedish company beat them to it. I would almost say that this remake is a point of honor, if that meant something to reptiles.

I have dealt with the ideological lies and distortions of *The Girl with the Dragon Tattoo* at length in my review of the Swedish movie. Here are a few bullet points:

❖ Stieg Larsson portrays Sweden as a country rife with violence and sadism toward women, when in fact Swedish women are by all objective standards some of the best off women in the world—thanks, of course, to the sufferance of Swedish men.

❖ Virtually all rape and violence against women in Sweden is committed not by Swedish men, but by non-white immigrants, mostly Muslims, whose immigration is being sponsored by Leftists like Stieg Larsson. In Larsson's world, however, the only immigrants are women who are raped and killed by Swedes.

❖ Sweden is one of the most Left-wing countries in Europe, where small, poorly funded nationalist groups are persecuted by Marxist thugs and hackers, including followers of Stieg Larsson. Larsson's Sweden, however, is menaced by wealthy, powerful Nazis who stalk and kill Jews for pleasure.

It is a tribute to Larsson's skill as a storyteller (or maybe just to his editors) that such an inverted world does not seem merely real, but compelling. It is a tribute to both Niels Oplev and David Fincher that such a vision has been brought to the screen twice without seeming like a parody of Left-wing paranoia and hysteria. But all the obvious talent, even virtuosity, that went into the book and movies is just candy coating on rat poison.

The Girl with the Dragon Tattoo in all its incarnations is the most repulsive and evil story in recent memory. No white person should pay a nickel to see this movie, which is an insult to our race produced by people who hate us. By pitting white women against white men, turning white children against their elders, and breaking down the barriers to race replacement by non-white immigration, *The Girl with the Dragon Tattoo* contributes to a far greater crime than the serial murders of Gottfried and Martin Vanger, namely the genocide of the white race.

In short, the true story *behind* this movie is far more horrifying than the false story *in* it.

Forget an R rating for sex, nudity, torture, and graphic violence. For Marxism, feminism, ethnomasochism, xenophilia, political correctness, all-round stupidity, scary Hollywood "Nazis," and anti-white genocidal intent, I rate this movie Zyklon B.

Counter-Currents/*North American New Right*,
December 27, 2011

The Girl Who Played with Fire

The Girl Who Played with Fire (2009) is the second novel/movie in the dismayingly popular *Millennium Trilogy* by the late Swedish communist and feminist Stieg Larsson. It is the sequel to *The Girl with the Dragon Tattoo*, which was recently remade in English directed by David Fincher. Assuming that Hollywood will remake all three Swedish films, we might as well get a sneak preview by taking a look at the Swedish sequels.

The basic cast of *The Girl Who Played with Fire* is the same as *The Girl with the Dragon Tattoo*, although the new movie was directed by Daniel Alfredson instead of Niels Arden Oplev. The look and style of both movies is very much the same.

I will now spoil the movie by summarizing the plot.

The Girl Who Played with Fire is set a year or so after the first movie. Lisbeth Salander, the "girl" of the title (although shouldn't womyn find "girl" demeaning?), has been living abroad but decides to return to Sweden. She stops by the home of her legal guardian, the lawyer Bjurman, who in the previous movie had a thing for tying her up and raping her. Lisbeth filmed one of these rapes and used it to blackmail Bjurman. To remind him of their arrangement, Lisbeth brandishes Bjurman's gun at him.

A short while later, Bjurman's gun is used to kill Bjurman and a young couple, Mia and Dag. Lisbeth's fingerprints are on the gun, so by an unlikely turn of events, she becomes a murder suspect.

The young couple were investigating human trafficking: the kidnapping of young Russian and East European women for sex slaves. (We see a Swedish journalist drooling as he rapes a young Russian who is tied to a bed.) Mia wrote her doctoral dissertation, *From Russia with Love*, on the subject. And, by another unlikely turn of events, her boyfriend Dag was writing about the same topic for *Millennium* magazine, a Left-wing journal that employs Mikael Blomkvist, Salander's partner in crime-solving in *The Girl with the Dragon Tattoo*.

With virtually no contact, Salander and Blomkvist work independently to solve the murders and clear Salander. (The two only see each other at the very end of the movie.)

But the improbabilities are just getting started. It turns out that the man running the human trafficking ring is Alexander Zalachenko, a Soviet GRU (military intelligence) defector who is living in Sweden. His triggerman is his son, Ronald Niedermann, a giant blonde thug who is incapable of feeling pain. (We're getting into Bond territory here.)

Zalachenko turns out to be Lisbeth Salander's father. (Niedermann is her half-brother.) Zalachenko regularly raped and assaulted Lisbeth's mother until she suffered permanent brain damage. Lisbeth, aged 12, then doused her father in gasoline and struck a match, leaving him disfigured and crippled.

Zalachenko's handlers in the Swedish government had Lisbeth confined to a mental institution for two years, where she spent more than half of the time tied to a bed (again with the bondage) by Dr. Peter Teleborian, a creepy psychiatrist with a penchant for underage girls. Lisbeth then was placed under the care of Holger Palmgren, a sympathetic social worker. Since she was deemed incapable of functioning as an adult, Bjurman the rapist was eventually appointed her legal guardian.

For no apparent reason, Zalachenko decides he wants Bjurman's files on Lisbeth, and Bjurman wants Lisbeth's blackmail video in exchange. For no apparent reason, Zalachenko dispatches Niedermann to kill Bjurman, even though his files on Lisbeth remain hidden. Then Niedermann kills the young couple who were working to expose his father's sex trafficking business. Niedermann also goes searching for Lisbeth.

Lisbeth takes up with one of her old lesbian flames, a blue-eyed woman with the unlikely name of Miriam Wu. We are treated to a long sex scene, which they refer to as "fucking," proving that sex education is not as advanced in Sweden as we were led to believe. To find Lisbeth, Niedermann abducts Wu but extracts no useful information from her, so he decides to burn her alive in a warehouse along with Paolo Roberto, a boxing instructor who comes to her rescue (they escape).

Lisbeth goes to Bjurman's weekend cottage and finds his secret files on her. Two motorcycle gangsters who work for Niedermann arrive to torch the place. Naturally, they decide to rape her. Lisbeth, using pepper spray, kickboxing, a taser, and a lot of grrrrrl power, overcomes the two toughs and escapes on one of their bikes.

Lisbeth finally tracks down Zalachenko and goes to confront him. She is captured. Niedermann digs a grave. Lisbeth tries to escape, but she is shot three times, once in the head, and buried. Yet she survives and manages to dig herself out with her cigarette case. She then plants an axe in Zalachenko's head and leg. With Zalachenko's gun, she chases off Niedermann. Only then does she collapse. Did I mention that the story is unlikely?

The movie ends with Blomkvist arriving to call the police and paramedics, who whisk both Lisbeth and Zalachenko, both of them still alive, off for treatment.

The Girl Who Played with Fire is a boring film. It clocks in at 2 hours, 9 minutes, but feels as long as *The Lord of the Rings*. There are many places in the film where a better director could create a great deal of suspense. But the real weakness is the underlying story, which is just a pulpy mishmash of one damn improbability after another, but filmed with the utmost seriousness.

Lisbeth Salander has to be the most unlikeable heroine in all of literature. Frankly, I cannot fathom the mind that would find her admirable. She strikes me as nothing but an embodiment of feminist paranoia and hatred. I can't even feel sorry for her, since her suffering is so unlikely.

Larsson does not make it clear if all Swedish women are tied up and raped by every third Swedish man, or if Lisbeth is just accident prone. But clearly he thinks that a very high percentage of Swedish men are rapists, hence their need to import victims. In reality, however, it is the rapists, not the victims who come from abroad: Virtually all the rape and sexual exploitation of Swedish women is the handiwork of non-white immigrants, primarily Muslims—imported and championed by feminist, multicultural Leftists like Stieg Larsson.

Furthermore, virtually all the trafficking in sex slaves in Russia and Eastern Europe is the handiwork of Jews, not ethnic Russians like Zalachenko. Larsson, moreover, was well aware of this connection, which we can infer from his studied attempt to invert reality. In one of the most interesting scene changes in the movie, we go from the discovery of the murdered couple to . . . a synagogue in Stockholm. A cell phone rings during the service, and a Jew answers. Is Larsson actually going to touch on the Jewish role in the sexual exploitation of Eastern European women? Of course not. This is Jan Bublanski, a policeman, one of the good guys, a real *Mensch* who is so concerned with helping his fellow man that he leaves his phone on in *shul*.

In spite of *The Millennium Trilogy*'s strident feminism, the truth is that for Larsson and the Left in general, the safety of white women is trumped every time it conflicts with the overriding agenda of preserving Jewish power and promoting white race replacement.

The Girl with the Dragon Tattoo is an evil film, but it still manages to be engrossing. This is also an evil film, filled with lies. But the story is so stupid, the villains so laughably cardboard, the heroes so wetly liberal, and the directing so boring that it is not a particularly apt propaganda vehicle. It will be interesting to see what Hollywood can make of it.

Counter-Currents/*North American New Right*,
February 3, 2012

The Girl Who Kicked the Hornet's Nest

The Girl Who Kicked the Hornet's Nest is the third novel and movie of the late Swedish Communist Stieg Larsson's *Millennium Trilogy*. The trilogy has sold 65 million copies as of December 2011, and in 2010, *The Girl Who Kicked the Hornet's Nest* was the best-selling novel in the US.

The Girl Who Kicked the Hornet's Nest is less a sequel to the second film, *The Girl Who Played with Fire*, than a continuation. It has the same director and cast, and it picks up immediately where the previous film left off. It feels like they merely changed reels.

At the end of *The Girl Who Played with Fire*, the "girl," lesbian autistic hacker Lisbeth Salander, was shot three times, once in the head, and buried alive by her father Alexander Zalachenko and her half-brother Ronald Niedermann. Zalachenko is a Soviet defector living under the protection of the Swedish government. He is a criminal kingpin involved in trafficking sex slaves, drugs, and arms from the former USSR. Niedermann, a giant blonde thug, is his father's chief enforcer.

Zalachenko routinely raped and abused Lisbeth's mother, finally leaving her crippled. To avenge her mother, the 12-year-old Lisbeth doused her father in gasoline and set him on fire, leaving him crippled and hideously disfigured. Zalachenko's handlers had Lisbeth committed to a mental hospital under the care of a child molester, Dr. Peter Teleborian. Later, when she came of age, she was declared legally incompetent and placed under the supervision of a creepy lawyer named Bjurman, who also raped her.

Naturally, when Lisbeth dug herself out of her grave (with a cigarette case), she took an axe and buried it Zalachenko's head and leg. Yet both survived, and at the beginning of the new film, they are being flown off for emergency medical treatment. We are treated to Lisbeth's brain surgery in gag-inducing detail. Then both father and daughter are wheeled off to separate rooms to recover. Both are looking at charges of attempted murder, among other things.

It turns out the Zalachenko's handlers work for a secret body within the Swedish government that is unknown even to the cabinet and Prime Minister. The group was created during a brief conservative government in the 1970s, and when the Social Democrats returned to power, nobody in the new cabinet was informed of their existence. This "deep state" apparatus is apparently the hornet's nest of the title, and Lisbeth Salander has them all abuzz.

Such "deep states" do exist, of course, but I have no doubt that its Swedish version does not take the form of a secret cabal of rapists and child molesters assembled by a conservative government. That is about as unlikely as the menacing Nazi serial killers of *The Girl with the Dragon Tattoo*—or every single event of *The Girl Who Played with Fire*, for that matter. Indeed, Larsson's Leftist fantasies about Sweden's deep state are refuted by his own story, which reveals the real Swedish deep state, which has a familiar blueprint.

The *Millennium* magazine from which the trilogy takes its name is clearly modeled on Larsson's own *Expo* magazine, which he founded in 1995 and edited until his death in 2004. *Expo* is an anti-racist, anti-fascist publication modeled on the UK's *Searchlight*. Like *Searchlight*, *Expo* has close connections with Jewish and Communist groups, as well as criminal elements (anti-fascist hackers, vandals, and thugs). *Expo* seeks to harass patriotic Swedes who resist the Jewish agenda of white race replacement.

In *The Girl Who Kicked the Hornet's Nest*, *Millennium* journalist Mikael Blomkvist (Larsson's fantasy alter ego) works to clear Lisbeth of the charges of attempted murder by exposing Zalachenko and his handlers and their conspiracy to imprison, silence, discredit, and ultimately kill Lisbeth. (When Zalachenko tries to blackmail his handlers, who are sick old men like himself, they dispatch a 78-year-old geezer to kill him in this hospital. He also tries to kill Lisbeth, but fails and kills himself to avoid capture. There are no guards on the rooms of either prisoner, by the way.)

When Blomkvist begins to uncover the hornet's nest, he is contacted by the Swedish secret police, who make him a consultant, using his research to take down the Right-wing cabal. The same pattern of Jewish-connected anti-racist, anti-fascist organizations working hand-in-hand with both secret police and criminal elements can be observed in the repression of white resistance to race replacement in the United States and the whole white world. It is a glimpse of the real "deep state": the Jewish-dominated anti-white power structure that has steered all white countries onto the path of demographic decline, miscegenation, and non-white immigration, which, if allowed to continue, will drive our race to extinction.

This revelation of the truth is, of course, rather shocking given Larsson's otherwise note-perfect politically correct inversions of reality. But even Homer nods from time to time. Surely if Larsson had lived to publish this book, he would have corrected this lapse.

Yes, the previous two novels/films that set the background story are ludicrous. Yes, Niedermann's relentless brutality is cartoonish. Yes, Lisbeth's acquittal makes no sense: she discredits the attempts to declare her insane, but this should not be sufficient for an acquittal on attempted murder charges. (Our plucky heroine's courtroom attire certainly does not help her case.) But as a story, *The Girl Who Kicked the Hornet's Nest* is by far the least implausible and most interesting chapter of the *Millennium Trilogy*. But that's not saying much. Moreover, the movie clocks in at 2-and-a-half hours, and you feel every minute of it. Even if it weren't evil, I couldn't recommend this movie. Life's just too short.

Counter-Currents/*North American New Right*,
February 7, 2011

300

Zack Snyder's *300*, based on Frank Miller's popular graphic novel of the same name, retells the story of King Leonidas of Sparta and his bodyguards, all but two of whom died defending the pass of Thermopylae against a vast Persian army in 480 B.C.E. (Since everyone should already know the story, I trust I will not be spoiling the ending.) In addition to the 300 Spartans, several thousand other Greeks also fought, and many of them died as well, but the Spartans are remembered for being particularly unsparing with their own lives.

The story of Thermopylae survives because it is retold. It is retold, because it inspires. It inspires because the Spartans did the right thing, which is rare and hard: they preferred collective freedom, even at the price of war, over peace purchased by submission to alien peoples and ways. Leonidas and his men, most of whom had sons to carry on their names, were willing to sacrifice their individual lives because they hoped to assure the collective survival and freedom of their families, including their common extended family, Sparta herself.

In the retelling, the tale of Thermopylae has inevitably been embroidered and mythologized. There are contradictions and gaps in the surviving accounts. But the real tale of Thermopylae is worth retelling, and it really can be retold. We can aim at complete historical accuracy, and where history does not record every detail, then we can aim at complete historical plausibility. Where our story cannot be true, it can at least be *likely*.

The only reason to set aside historical accuracy is because one wishes to use Thermopylae to promote values the Spartans would have found alien and repellent. This was done during the French Revolution, when the image of the aristocratic Spartans was used to promote egalitarianism. It is also done in Snyder's *300*, where historical accuracy and plausibility are cast to the winds to pursue another agenda.

The question, though, is: Whose agenda?

The reason so many find *300* a shocking, perplexing movie

is that the most straightforward interpretation is as White Nationalist race war propaganda in the vein of William Pierce's *The Turner Diaries*.

Although director Snyder preserves Miller's sepia and red dominated color palate, there can be no confusion about the races of the protagonists. The Spartans are portrayed as Nordic Europeans, physically magnificent and beautiful Nordics, which is historically accurate. The Persians, however, are portrayed as entirely non-white. Some of them are even non-human. Most of them are blacks and racially indeterminate mongrels. The Persian Emperor Xerxes is portrayed by a towering mulatto. The Persian Immortals are dressed like ninjas, and when their masks are removed, they look like orcs from *The Lord of the Rings* movies.

But clearly *300* was not made to promote White Nationalism. So what is its real agenda? To answer that question, we have to look at Frank Miller's original graphic novel. My first impression was that *300* is the work of a Jewish neoconservative. But Miller is apparently not a Jew. He was raised a Catholic. Upon closer inspection, *300* reads like the work of an Objectivist: "mysticism" is disdained, "reason" and "freedom" are exalted. In terms of their foreign policy, Objectivists are hyperbellicose Zionists who disdain the neoconservatives as too soft, sentimental, and unprincipled.

Now that Iraq has been devastated at American expense, Iran is at the top of the Zionist hit list. Thus it makes perfect sense to create a graphic novel and a movie about European resistance to a Persian invasion. Thus *300* plays the same role as Oliver Stone's *Alexander*, which also has a clear Zionist war propaganda agenda.

In the original graphic novel, the struggle between the Spartans and the Persians cannot be interpreted as a race war, simply because *all* the characters, even the Spartans, look like Negroes or Negroid mongrels. Why Miller (along with colorist Lynn Varley) chose this mode of portrayal is hard to fathom. My guess is that their image of the ancients is based on their ideal audience, the "tan everyman," the brown mongrel race that would emerge through universal miscegenation, the ideal citizen of a universal homogeneous state.

In addition to Miller's repugnant racial, political, and philosophical agenda, his dialogue is, well, what you would expect from a comic book, rarely rising above the pedestrian, anachronistic, and clichéd.

Yes, there are some good bits here and there, particularly Miller's treatment of Ephialtes, a hunchback who would have been discarded by the Spartans as an infant, but who was saved by his tenderhearted parents. Ephialtes offers his services to Leonidas, but Leonidas rejects him as unfit to fight (with all compassion consistent with being truthful). Leonidas suggests that he is capable of tending the wounded and bringing water to the warriors, but Ephialtes, in a narcissistic rage, instead betrays the Spartans to their doom. Xerxes says that Leonidas was cruel to demand that Ephialtes stand. Xerxes, out of kindness, demands only that he kneel. Leonidas, when he sees that Ephialtes has betrayed him, wishes that he live forever—for a dishonorable life is a far worse fate than an honorable death. It is pure Nietzsche, by way of Ayn Rand, but it is also magnificently Greek, and a fundamental rejection of Christian and liberal values.

300 is not just an insult to Leonidas and the Spartans. It is an insult to the taste and intelligence of anyone with a basic knowledge of history and literature.

Director Zack Snyder (who is not Jewish either) was artist enough to cast the Spartans as Europeans, but for some reason he did not tamper with Miller's vision of the Persians. Perhaps it appealed to his imagination as a monster movie director.

Snyder, by the way, is so talented a director that one occasionally forgets how stupid and offensive the script is.

To the naïve viewer (and face it, that is practically everyone these days), *300* is a visually stunning ballet of slaughter. It is a poetic celebration of the love of comrades, the hatred of enemies, the sublimity of self-sacrifice, and plain old ripped, shredded, berserk, rampaging machismo.

The movie also explains and justifies the brutal eugenic selection and military training of the Spartans. If Sparta still existed, this movie would have sent waves of young men seeking to enlist in its military, just as *Full Metal Jacket* turned into a recruitment movie for the Marines.

And because of Snyder's casting choices, Miller's abstractions about reason and mysticism make scarcely any impression compared to the stark confrontation of Europeans against the invading hordes of Africa and the Near East.

The Persians of *300* do not resemble ancient Persians at all. Nor do they resemble modern Persians so much as the blacks, Arabs, and North Africans who make up the bulk of Europe's Muslim invaders.

If in ten or twenty years, Europe explodes into race war and expels the Muslims, the consciousness of the young men who fight will be shaped more by the images of Zack Snyder's Spartans than by almost forgotten figures like Charles Martel.

The sacrifice of Leonidas and the 300 inspired the Greeks to unite and repel the Persian invasion. May they continue to inspire our people to ever newer victories.

Counter-Currents/*North American New Right*,
January 7, 2011

Gangs of New York

I finally saw *Gangs of New York*, and I wish that I had gone much sooner. *Gangs* is an absolutely magnificent movie, the best movie I have seen since *The Two Towers*. It is Martin Scorsese's best movie—ever. Better even than *Taxi Driver*, which has been my favorite of his films until now. But *Gangs* is now closing its run in theaters all over the country, so see it if you still have the chance, for it is an unforgettable experience on the big screen.

I am in general agreement with Erik Meyer's letter about *Gangs* posted on VDARE, and I recommend that you read it.[1]

Gangs is the story of the conflict between two criminals, Bill "the Butcher" Cutting (Daniel Day-Lewis) and Amsterdam Vallon (Leonardo DiCaprio), in New York's "Five Points" during the American Civil War. Bill the Butcher is the head of the "Native Americans" gang, fighting for the interests of those who descended from the original settlers and founders of the United States against recent immigrants, primarily from Ireland. The immigrants are represented by the "Dead Rabbits," a gang led by "Priest" Vallon (Liam Neeson).

The prologue of *Gangs* is set around fourteen years before the main story. The Dead Rabbits and the Native Americans meet to settle, by the "ancient laws of combat," who has control over Five Points. The battle is the most savage and gut-wrenching I have seen on screen since *Braveheart*. In the end Priest Vallon is mortally wounded and then dispatched by Bill the Butcher while young Amsterdam Vallon looks on in horror. Orphaned, he is taken to a reformatory, where he nurses his resentment, gets into lots of fights, and dreams of revenge.

All grown up, Amsterdam returns to New York, joins Bill the Butcher's gang, and gains first his trust and then his love, becoming the son he never had. And the love of Bill the Butcher is not something to be spurned. Not because he is a dangerous criminal who might take revenge, but because he is a truly hero-

---

[1] http://www.vdare.com/letters/tl_010503.htm

ic and noble man, one of the most remarkable characters in film and literature—ever. And his portrayal by Daniel Day-Lewis is one of the greatest film performances—ever. (Given the mounting exposure of Jewish evil in the world, it only makes sense that Lewis and Scorsese were passed over in the Oscars. Adrien Brody received the Best Actor and Roman Polanski the Best Director Oscars for what must be the six millionth Holocaust flick, *The Pianist*.)

Torn between his feelings for Bill the Butcher, who is the greatest man he has ever met, and the dead father he barely knew, Amsterdam chooses revenge. Not that Amsterdam is unable to appreciate Bill the Butcher's greatness. But in the end he succumbs to his own smallness. His chosen method of revenge is equally small and cowardly. Instead of meeting Bill the Butcher in open combat, as "Priest" Vallon did, Amsterdam tries to assassinate the Butcher "like a sneak thief" with a throwing knife while he is celebrating the anniversary of his victory over the Priest.

It is an act of revenge that dishonors not only Amsterdam, but also his father, who was cut from the same noble stuff as Bill the Butcher. The Butcher respects him as the "only man he ever killed worth remembering." It is a brutal irony that Priest Vallon was better honored by the man who killed him than by the son who avenged him.

The assassination fails, and Bill the Butcher leaves Amsterdam alive, to experience the shame of his cowardice and defeat, and perhaps to recover his honor, just as "Priest" Vallon once let a defeated Bill the Butcher live to redeem himself. The Butcher's mistake is that such tactics only work against honorable men, and Amsterdam Vallon is not an honorable man. Amsterdam Vallon is supposed to be the hero of this film, but he is utterly despicable, and he never redeems himself in the end.

Gangs proves that director Scorsese is a genius of subversion. Like Travis Bickle in *Taxi Driver*, Bill the Butcher presents a coherent and compelling critique of the society of his time. And like Travis Bickle, Bill the Butcher is portrayed as a psychopath and a criminal. But both Bickle and the Butcher are alienated and "maladjusted" because they are idealists frustrated by the corruption of the world around them. They take to violence only because society falls short of their ideals. They see violence as the only way to restore the proper order of things. They are instruments of a higher justice, a justice that requires the system be overthrown.

Hollywood would never allow the sentiments of Travis Bickle or Bill the Butcher to be uttered by heroes, but they think it safe to put them in the mouths of villains. Smugly conventional people will, of course, dismiss anything said by a criminal or a "psycho," no matter how coherent and compelling. But people with minds accept the truth no matter who speaks it. People of honor admire heroism no matter who displays it.

Bill the Butcher is a far more articulate hero than Travis Bickle, and *Gangs* presents a far more complex criticism of American society than *Taxi Driver*. According to Bill the Butcher, America is not an "idea" like freedom or equality. It is not a political or economic "system" like capitalism or democracy. America is an organic community, a community of blood: a community purchased by the blood of its founders to safeguard the blood of their posterity. Bill the Butcher's father spilled his blood fighting for America. Bill the Butcher was born in this country. And that, to his mind, should count for something. He has a birthright, a blood right, not a mere abstract "human" right that does not distinguish him from a Hottentot or a Papuan.

Because of his philosophy of Blood and Soil, Bill the Butcher is opposed to immigration. He sees immigration for what it was then, and what it is now: a tool by which raceless, rootless men dispossess Americans of their birthrights. In *Gangs* the two representatives of this type are Abraham Lincoln and Boss Tweed.

In a brilliant sequence, Scorsese shows how Lincoln's men took desperate young Irishmen right off one boat, enlisted them in the Union army to dispossess Southerners of their birthrights, and then loaded them onto another boat—while at the same time offloading coffin upon coffin of his victims. This is why Bill the Butcher throws a knife into a poster of Lincoln and starts a riot at a performance of *Uncle Tom's Cabin*. He sees that Lincoln's artificial "Union" devoted to the "proposition" of equality is the mortal enemy of an organic community based on blood. The blood of white men is more valuable than the blood of blacks. So there is no reason for white men to die for the freedom of blacks.

Boss Tweed uses immigrant votes to defeat nativist candidates, running the same people through the polls again and again until the votes cast outnumber the potential voters. Don't laugh. That is how your votes are being nullified today.

Another category of raceless profiteers on immigration are the businessmen who use it to depress wages, paying an Irishman a nickel to do the job an American once did for a dollar. Nothing, apparently, has changed.

The main objects of Bill the Butcher's wrath are the Irish, but it is clear that he opposes the Irish because they are immigrants, not the immigrants because they are Irish. Indeed, the man in the film he admires most is Priest Vallon, and he employs Irishmen in his gang. This is important to note, because one effect of *Gangs* is to exacerbate Irish resentment against the American establishment and promote a mindless attachment to open borders, because, after all, the Irish were unwelcome immigrants too. Just for the record: I love Irish people, Irish literature, and Irish folk music. But that does not blind me to what I like to call "the Irish Question."

There is an Irish Question for the same reason that there is a Jewish Question: the Irish are good at holding grudges, and they have carried their grudge against the English to America, directing it against the White Anglo-Saxon Protestants who founded and used to run this country. The divisive presence of the Irish was an important factor in the rise of our present Jew-dominated system, and although the Irish are slated for eventual extermination along with the rest of us, they still enjoy a higher status in the propasphere than any other white ethnic group.

That's why Americans all celebrate Saint Patrick's Day, but not Saint George's Day. That's why on television and in the movies so many of the positive white characters (crusading liberal attorneys, meddling social workers, sensitive cops, and all manner of career girls) have Irish names. That's why the multicultural "Rainbow Confederates" of the League of the South promote the myth of a "Celtic" Confederacy in a pathetic attempt to align themselves with a Jew-approved white ethnic category, which in effect would assure them only of being on the *last* cattle car to the extermination camps.

In this context, Amsterdam Vallon can be seen, not merely as an individual Irishman, but as a symbol of the Irish Question. He has inherited a grudge. He is sick with self-pity and eaten up by resentment. He tosses his Bible in the river when released from the reformatory, but uses the Catholic Church as a rallying place when it suits him politically. He even prays for victory. In his resentment against Bill the Butcher, the American of Blood and Soil, he allows himself to be used by Boss Tweed, the rootless System man, to strip Americans of their birthrights. He is too stupid, or too blinded by his own pettiness, to see that the system he is aiding will in the end destroy him and his kind too.

The fact that the same System is at war with both Americans and immigrants is underscored by the backdrop of the film's climax: the great New York draft riots of 1863. When the System began to draft men into the Union army, but allowed the rich to buy exemptions, the poor rioted. Politicians and blacks were lynched; the military was called in to restore order; thousands were killed. Scorsese's handling of the riots is brilliant.[2]

Gangs has been criticized because the riots overwhelm and literally obscure the battle between Bill the Butcher and Amsterdam Vallon. But that's the point. The great tragedy of this film is the tragedy of the white race as a whole: We are divided by language, culture, religion, and ancient, senseless grudges, which drive the best of us — the Bill the Butchers and Priest Vallons — to slaughter each other, when we should be uniting to destroy the System that was, and still is, destroying us.

VNN, March 30, 2003

---

[2] The riot scenes were especially satisfying to me because Scorsese smashes and burns the sort of props and accessories that marred his worst movie, *The Age of Innocence*. These items were so obtrusive that the film seemed like a cross between Merchant-Ivory and the Home Shopping Network.

A History of Violence

David Cronenberg's *A History of Violence* (New Line Cinema, 2005) is truly a superb movie, with a tight and economical script (the whole story is told in 96 minutes), a remarkably subtle and gripping performance by Viggo Mortensen (his best ever, in my opinion), excellent performances from the rest of the cast, and an unostentatiously elegant directorial style (unmarred by the middlebrow pretentiousness and penchant for the juvenile and repulsive that ruin most of Cronenberg's movies).

The hero of *A History of Violence* is Tom Stall, played by Viggo Mortensen. As the movie opens, Stall is portrayed as very much a white everyman. He is a family man with a wife (Edie, played by Maria Bello) and two children (Jack, played by Ashton Holmes, and Sarah, played by Heidi Hayes). He lives in Millbrook, Indiana, a small, apparently entirely white town in the Midwest. (Only one black appears, a TV news reporter from out of town.)

Tom is middle class, but a little above middle, as he owns a small business (a diner, where he mans the counter, coffee pot, and cash register), and his wife Edie is a small-town lawyer. Both Tom and Edie wear crosses around their necks, which are clearly visible in several scenes, so it is impossible to mistake them for anything but Christians.

Like a lot of American men today, Tom is a bit of a wimp. Physically, he is not soft or effeminate, but fit and manly. Yet his manner is hesitant and self-deprecating, his speech laconic and soft, his voice sometimes high-pitched and pleading. His wife, by contrast, is articulate, outspoken, and confident. In many scenes, she does the talking for Tom. Tom is sexually passive while his wife is sexually aggressive. In a rather subtle touch, throughout most of the movie Tom cannot get his masculine pickup truck to start, so his wife drives him to work in her maternal station wagon.

The Stalls' teenage son is a bit of a wimp too. Like his father, he has an athletic physique and athletic ability, but not an athlete's self-confidence. He is bullied by some jocks, who call him a "fag," and he replies only with sarcasm. His verbal self-confidence comes from his mother the lawyer.

But we see there is more to Tom than meets the eye when two thugs hold up his diner at closing time. (The robbers have already been established as sadistic killers.) When it becomes apparent that they want to take more than just money, Tom, in a thrilling, cathartic explosion of violence, kills them both.

Immediately, Tom is hailed by the news media as a hero, but he shuns the acclaim and attention in his soft-spoken, self-deprecating manner. He just wants life to go back to normal. Unfortunately, some people just won't let him.

A few days later, when the diner has reopened, three well-dressed but sinister out-of-towners drop by. The leader, Carl Fogarty (played by Ed Harris), has a hideously scarred face. Fogarty insists that Tom Stall is actually named Joey Cusak, that he is from Philadelphia, and that they have met before. Tom, somewhat flustered, denies their allegations. Then Edie steps in and tells them firmly to leave.

Once the trio departs, Edie calls the Sheriff, who pulls the men over and tells them to leave town. Then he looks into their identities. They are gangsters from Philadelphia with long criminal records. Suspense mounts as Fogarty and his men stalk and menace the Stall family. Fogarty tells Edie that Tom was involved in organized crime (his brother Richie Cusak is a big mobster), that Tom has killed before, and that it was Tom who scarred his face and blinded him in one eye.

Meanwhile, Jack Stall, no doubt imitating his father's heroism in the diner, decides to fight back against the bullies who have been picking on him. He is suspended and sent home from school. Tom first rebukes his son for using violence. He tells him that in their family they do not solve problems by hitting people. Jack hurls back, "No, in this family we kill them." Stung, Tom slaps Jack's face, and Jack storms out of the house.

Jack returns a while later as a hostage of Fogarty and his men. Fogarty offers to trade Jack for his father. He tells Tom that he wants to take him to Philadelphia and on a ride "down memory lane." Both destinations sound ominous.

Tom complies long enough to secure Jack's release. Then he fights. Tom handily kills Fogarty's two goons, but is wounded by Fogarty. As he lies on the ground, Fogarty towering over him about to deliver the *coup de grâce*, Tom says that he should have killed Fogarty back in Philadelphia when he had the chance. So Tom is Joey after all. But before Fogarty can fire, he is felled from behind by a shotgun blast. It is Jack. He solved the problem, Stall style.

Edie and Jack are naturally horrified to discover that Tom Stall is really Joey Cusak, a mob-connected killer. Jack responds with more smart talk. Edie's reaction runs the gamut from retching (the only scene that really rings false) to weeping and screaming to standing up for her husband when the Sheriff begins asking questions.

Tom, for his part, makes it clear that he did more than merely change his name. It was a process of psychological death and rebirth. He says he went out to the desert (symbolically a place of purification) and killed Joey, and he was only fully reborn when he married Edie. This is a very significant point, for the whole film dwells on the contrast between bands of unmarried men and married men with families, and what makes the transition possible.

But everyone, including Tom himself, has reason to be glad that Joey was not killed off in the desert. It is Joey who saved the customers and staff of Stall's diner. It is Joey who saved the Stall family from Fogarty. It is also Joey who gave Jack the strength to stand up for himself and his family, even to the point of killing Fogarty.

Edie, moreover, finds Joey sexually attractive. When a heated argument turns suddenly violent, Edie finds it arousing. Although it is Edie who first turns the tussle in a sexual direction, overall the scene reverses the couple's earlier lovemaking, where Edie is active and Tom passive. The scene is psychologically plausible, totally politically incorrect, and just plain hot. But in the end, Joey still spends the night on the couch.

Joey is awakened by a phone call from his brother Richie, who asks him to come to Philadelphia. The alternative is that

Richie come there, which would endanger the family. So, in the dead of night, Joey gets in his pickup truck (which he can now get started) and heads to Philadelphia.

The climax of the movie is the meeting of Joey and Richie (in a reptilian portrayal by William Hurt) in a posh suburban mansion. We learn that Joey fled Philadelphia after savagely beating Carl Fogarty and killing some of his men. Fogarty was a "made man" in the mob, so Richie's own career was impeded by his brother's impulsive violence. (As Joey points out, however, Richie seems to have done well for himself anyway.)

The bulk of their conversation deals with family.

First, Richie makes it clear that monogamy holds no charms for him. He can't see how one woman can make him want to give up all the others. Joey, however, understands. It is how he was transformed from "Crazy Joey," the ultra-violent outcast from his own criminal *Männerbund*, into a responsible family man who would not only live beyond his violent youth, but beyond his own death through his children.

Second, Joey explains that he fled Philadelphia after beating Fogarty because he thought Richie would choose career over family, avenging Fogarty rather than protecting his brother. Richie admits that he was right.

Joey seems fully cognizant that no matter how much he has changed (and it was less than he thought), his brother has not changed at all. Still, Joey's hope that he can mend his relationship with his brother is touchingly palpable. But when Richie reminisces about the time he tried to strangle Joey in his crib and then adds as an aside, "I guess all kids do that," the effect is slightly comical but so inhuman that it makes a mockery of Joey's hopes.

When Richie signals to one of his henchmen to strangle Joey, there is another explosion of violence, leaving Richie and four henchmen dead.

The movie ends with Joey's return home at dinnertime on a dark autumn evening. The scene is tense. No words are spoken. But the tension begins to ease when Sarah sets a place at the table for her father. He sits down, the circle mended, and Edie slowly raises her eyes to look into Tom's.

We are left with some hope that Tom is finally free of his past, that his family is safe, and that they will find a way of living with Joey rather than trying to bury him again in the desert.

A History of Violence is a meditation on the inherent connection between manliness and the capacity for violence. The movie clearly shows the necessity of domesticating wolf packs of young violent males (the bullying jocks, the two wandering killers, the Philadelphia mafia) who struggle to establish dominance hierarchies and egg one another on to challenge authority, transgress boundaries, and use and discard females. Unless such young men can form families and follow laws, society — and much of the human race — will perish.

But what sets *A History of Violence* apart, and makes it a remarkable movie, is that it also shows that we must civilize young men without emasculating them, because the masculine capacity for violence is also what protects the family and social order from unattached, predatory males. It is strong, responsible, manly men — not Hollywood's ball-busting female cops, cat-suited karate girls, and other silly "strong women" clichés; not academia's sensitivity training, candlelight vigils, and feminist scolds — that are the true bulwark of civilization. This is hardly the sort of message delivered by most movies today.

I highly recommend *A History of Violence*. It is a pro-family movie that you definitely will *not* want to show the whole family.

The Occidental Observer, November 17, 2007

Mishima:
A Life in Four Chapters

Similar things happen in the United States too: an alienated, bookish radical Right-winger takes up weight-lifting and martial arts, creates a private militia, dreams of overthrowing the government, then dies in a spectacular, suicidal, and apparently pointless confrontation with the state. In the United States, however, such people are easily dismissed as "kooks" and "losers." However, when it happened in Japan, the protagonist, Yukio Mishima, was one of the nation's most famous and respected novelists.

Director Paul Schrader's 1985 movie, *Mishima: A Life in Four Chapters*, is an excellent introduction to Mishima's life and work. It is by far the best movie about an artist I have ever seen. It is also surely the most sympathetic film portrayal of a figure who was essentially a fascist, maybe since *Triumph of the Will*.

Paul Schrader, of German Calvinist descent, is famous as the writer or co-writer of the screenplays of Martin Scorsese's *Taxi Driver*, *Raging Bull*, *The Last Temptation of Christ*, and *Bringing Out the Dead*. His other screenplays include Brian De Palma's *Obsession*, Peter Weir's *The Mosquito Coast*, and his own *American Gigolo*. Other movies directed by Schrader include the near-dreadful remake of *Cat People* and the brilliant *Auto Focus*, a biopic about a very different sort of artist, Bob Crane. It is so creepy that I will never watch it again, even though it is a masterpiece.

Mishima, however, is Schrader's best film. He also co-wrote the screenplay with his brother Leonard. (The score, moreover, is the best thing ever written by Philip Glass.)

The narrative frame of the movie is Mishima's last day, which is filmed in realistic color. The story of his life is told in black and white flashbacks, intercut with dramatizations of parts of three of Mishima's novels, *The Temple of the Golden Pavilion*, *Kyoko's House*, and *Runaway Horses*, which are filmed on unrealistic stage sets in lavish Technicolor.

Yukio Mishima was a very, very, very sensitive child. Born Kimitake Hiraoke in 1925 to an upper middle class family with samurai ancestry, he was taken from his mother by his grandmother, who kept him indoors, told him that he was physically fragile, prevented him from playing with other boys, and made him her factotum until she died when he was twelve. Then he returned to his parents.

Highly intelligent and convinced of his physical frailty, Mishima became bookish and introverted: a reader and a writer, a poet and a dreamer. He wrote his first short stories at age 12. Denied an outlet for healthy, boyish aggression, he became a masochist. He was also homosexual.

Imbued with samurai tradition, he longed to fight in the Second World War and die for the Emperor, but he was rejected as physically unfit for duty, a source of life-long self-reproach. He had a cold when he reported for his physical, and he later claimed that out of cowardice he exaggerated his symptoms so the doctor thought he had tuberculosis.

Mishima's first book was published when he 19. He wrote at least 100 books—40 novels, 20 collections of short stories, 20 plays (including a screenplay and an opera libretto), and 20-odd book-length essays and collections of essays—before his death at age 45. He also dabbled in acting and directing.

The Temple of the Golden Pavilion

Schrader's dramatization of Mishima's 1956 novel *The Temple of the Golden Pavilion* focuses on the author's Nietzschean exploration of the role of physiognomy and will to power in the origin of values. Nietzsche believed that all organisms have will to power, even sickly and botched ones. In the realm of values, will to power manifests itself particularly in a desire to think well of oneself. A healthy organism affirms itself by positing values that affirm its nature. The healthy affirm health, strength, beauty, and power. They despise the sickly, weak, and ugly.

But sickly organisms have will to power too. They affirm themselves by positing values based on their natures, values that cast them in a positive light and cast healthy organisms in a negative light. This is the origin of ascetic and "spiritual" values, as well as the Christian values of the Sermon on the Mount, which Nietzsche calls "slave morality."

The Temple of the Golden Pavilion is loosely based on the burning of the Reliquary (or Golden Pavilion) of Kinkaku-ji in Kyoto by a deranged Buddhist acolyte in 1950. In Mishima's story, the arson is committed by Mizoguchi, an acolyte afflicted with ugliness and a stutter. The acolyte recognizes the beauty of the Golden Pavilion, but also hates it, because its beauty magnifies his deformities.

Mizoguchi's clubfooted friend Kashiwagi tries to teach Mizoguchi to use his disabilities to arouse women's pity and exploit it to get sex. Kashiwagi can use his disability because he lacks pride and will to power. Mizoguchi, however, cannot enjoy beauty by means of self-abasement. He cannot own his imperfections. The vision of the Golden Pavilion prevents him. He can like himself only if the Golden Pavilion is destroyed, thus he sets it ablaze.

In Nietzsche's terms, the destruction of the Golden Pavilion is an act of transvaluation. The beauty that oppresses Mizoguchi must be destroyed. For Nietzsche, this act of destruction serves to create a space for new values that will allow him to affirm his disability, just as the destruction of aristocratic values creates a space for slave morality.

Schrader includes this dramatization of *The Temple of the Golden Pavilion* to illustrate Mishima's exploration of his own youthful nihilism. Short even by Japanese standards (5'1"), skinny, physically frail, Mishima envied and eroticized the bodies of healthier boys, an eroticism that Mishima's *Confessions of a Mask* clearly indicates was tinged with masochistic self-hatred and sadistic fantasies of brutality and murder. (Mishima first became sexually aroused at a photograph of a painting of the martyrdom of Saint Sebastian.)

Self-Transformation

The Temple of the Golden Pavilion, however, is a look backwards, at paths Mishima could understand but not follow. Unlike Kashiwagi, Mishima could not own his physical imperfections. Unlike Mizoguchi, he could not annihilate the ideal of beauty just to feel good about himself. This left Mishima with only one choice: to remake his body according to the ideal of physical beauty. Thus in 1955, Mishima started lifting weights, with impressive results. He also took up kendo and karate.

Mishima documented his physical transformation with a very un-Japanese exhibitionism. He posed frequently for photographers, producing a book, *Ordeal by Roses* (1963), in collaboration with photographer Eikoh Hosoe. Mishima also posed in *Young Samurai: Bodybuilders of Japan* and *OTOKO: Photo Studies of the Young Japanese Male* by Tamotsu Yatō. His acting work was also an extension of this exhibitionism, as was his dandyism. When he wasn't posing nude or in a loincloth, his clothes were almost exclusively Western. He dressed up like James Bond and dressed down like James Dean.

In 1958, his body and self-confidence transformed, Mishima married Yoko Sugiyama. It was an arranged marriage. They had two children. (Among Mishima's requirements for a wife was that she have no interest in his work and that she be shorter than him. As an indication of his social circles, Mishima had earlier considered Michiko Shōda as a possible bride. She went on to marry Crown Prince Akihito and is now Empress of Japan.)

In 1959, Mishima built a house in an entirely Western style. Following the Nietzschean principle that every authentic culture has an integrity and unity of style, Mishima rejected multiculturalism, including mixing Japanese and Western lifestyles. Since he could not live in an entirely Japanese house, he chose to live in an entirely Western one, where he could "sit on rococo furniture wearing Levis and an aloha shirt."

Kyoko's House

The second Mishima novel Schrader dramatizes is *Kyoko's House* (1959), which cries out for an English translation. According to the literature, *Kyoko's House* is an exploration of Mishima's own psyche, aspects of which are concretized in the four main characters: a boxer, who represents Mishima's new-found athleticism; a painter, who represents his creative side; a businessman, who like Mishima lives an outwardly conventional life but rejects postwar Japanese society; and an actor, who represents his narcissism.

Schrader focuses only on the story of the actor, who takes up bodybuilding when humiliated by a gangster sent to intimidate his mother, who was in debt to loan sharks. The moneylender turns out to be a woman. She offers to cancel the loan if the actor sells himself to her.

The narcissist, whose sense of reality is based on the impression he makes in the eyes of others, realizes that even his newly acquired muscles are not real to him. The realization comes when his lover, on a sadistic whim, cuts his skin with a razor. In physical pain, he finds a sense of reality otherwise unavailable due to his personality disorder. Their sexual relationship takes a sadomasochistic turn that culminates in a suicide pact — foreshadowing Mishima's own end.

Having put so much of himself into *Kyoko's House*, Mishima was deeply wounded by its commercial and critical failure. Schrader had first wanted to dramatize Mishima's *Forbidden Colors*, his novel about Japan's homosexual subculture, but Mishima's widow refused permission. (She denied that Mishima had any homosexual proclivities.) But it is just as well. From what I can gather, *Kyoko's House* is a far better novel than *Forbidden Colors*.

Schrader did not dramatize the story of the boxer in *Kyoko's House*, but it also foreshadows Mishima's life as well. After one of his hands is shattered in a fight, the boxer becomes involved in Right-wing politics. Mishima makes it quite clear that the boxer's political commitment is not based on ideology, but on a physically ruined man's desire for an experience of self-transcendence and sublimity.

The businessman's outlook is also important for understanding Mishima's life and outlook. He thinks postwar Japan is a spiritual void in which prosperity, materialism, peace, and resolute amnesia about the war years have sapped life of authenticity, which requires that one face death, something that was omnipresent during the war.

Authenticity through awareness of death, pain as an encounter with reality, and Right-wing politics as a form of self-transcendence (or therapy): *Kyoko's House* maps out the trajectory of the rest of Mishima's life.

MISHIMA'S POLITICAL TURN

Mishima, like many Western Right-wingers, saw tradition as a third way between capitalism and socialism, which are essentially identical in their materialistic ends and their scientific and technological means. He always had Right-wing tendencies, but his writings in the 1940s and 1950s were absorbed (self-absorbed, truth be told) with personal moral and psychological issues.

Like many Japanese, however, Mishima became increasingly alarmed by the corruptions of postwar consumer society. He saw the samurai tradition as an aristocratic alternative to massification, a spiritual alternative to materialism. He saw the Japanese military and the Emperor as guardians of this tradition. But these guardians had already made too many compromises with modernity. Mishima was particularly critical of the Emperor's renunciation of divinity at the end of the Second World War. In his writings and actions in the last decade of his life, Mishima sought to call the Emperor and the military back to their mission as guardians of Japanese tradition.

In the fall of 1960, Mishima wrote "Patriotism," a short story about the aftermath of the "Ni Ni Roku Incident" of February 1936, an attempted *coup d'état* by junior officers of the Imperial Army who assassinated several political leaders. The officers wished the government to address widespread poverty caused by the worldwide Great Depression. The coup was cast as an attempt to restore the absolute power of the Emperor, but he regarded it as a rebellion and ordered it crushed.

Mishima's story focuses on Lieutenant Shinji Takeyama and his young wife, Reiko. The Lieutenant did not take part in the coup but was friends with the participants. He is ordered to help suppress it. Torn between loyalty to the Emperor and loyalty to his friends, he chooses to commit suicide by self-disembowelment after a night of love-making. Reiko joins him in death.

Mishima published "Patriotism" in 1961. In 1965, he directed and starred in 28-minute film adaptation which he first released in France. The film of *Patriotism* is erotic, chilling, and cringe-inducingly graphic (people regularly fainted when they saw it in theaters). In retrospect, it seems like merely a rehearsal for Mishima's eventual suicide. The music, fittingly, is the *Liebestod* (Love-Death) from Wagner's *Tristan und Isolde*. Mishima's widow locked up the film after her husband's death. After her death, it was released on DVD by the Criterion Collection. (Mishima also committed suicide on screen in Hideo Gosha's 1969 film *Tenchu!*)

Schrader shows bits of the filming of *Patriotism* and also dramatizes a very similar episode from *Runaway Horses* (1969), the second volume of Mishima's *The Sea of Fertility* quartet (1968–1970). *The Sea of Fertility* is a panorama of Japan's traumatic crash course in modernization, spanning the years 1912 to 1975, narrating the life of Shigekuni Honda, who becomes a wealthy and widely-traveled jurist.

Runaway Horses, set in 1932–1933, is the story of Isao Iinuma, a Right-wing student who seeks the alliance of the military to plot a rebellion in 1932. The goal is to topple capitalism and restore absolute Imperial rule by simultaneously assassinating the heads of industry and the government and torching the Bank of Japan. The plot is foiled, but when Isao is released from prison, he carries out his part of the mission anyway, assassinating his target. The assassination, of course, is politically futile, but Isao feels honor-bound to carry out his mission. He then commits *hari-kiri*.

Isao's plot is clearly based on the Ni Ni Roku Incident. The novel also tells the story of the Samurai insurrection in Kunamoto in 1876. But it would be a mistake to conclude that Mishima put his hope in a successful military coup as the most likely path to a renewal of Japanese tradition. Mishima's focus was on the ritual suicides of the defeated rebels.

The Way of the Samurai

Japan had 300 years of peace under the Tokugawa Shogunate. Conflict had been outlawed; history in the Hegelian sense had been ended. Yet the arts and culture flourished, and the Japanese had not been reduced to a mass of dehumanized and degraded producer-consumers. The cause of this was the persistence of the samurai ethic.

The samurai, of course, like all aristocrats, prefer death to dishonor, and when prevented from demonstrating this on the battlefield, they demonstrated it instead through ritual suicide. They also demonstrated their contempt of material necessity through the cultivation of luxury and refinement. The cultural supremacy of the ideal of the honor suicide served as a bulwark protecting high culture against degeneration into bourgeois consumer culture, which springs from an opposing hierarchy of values that prizes life, comfort, and security over honor.

Mishima's cultural-political project makes the most sense if we view it not as an attempt to return to militarism, but as an attempt to uphold or revive the samurai ethic in postwar Japan so that it could play the same conservative role as it did under the 300-year peace of the Shogunate. (Mishima's outlook would then be very similar to that of Alexandre Kojève, who in his *Introduction to the Reading of Hegel* claimed that Japan under the Shogunate showed how we might retain our humanity at the end of history through an aristocratic culture that rested on the cultural ideal of a "purely gratuitous suicide.")

Mishima produced a spate of political books and essays in the 1960s, most of which have remained untranslated. Two of the most important, however, are available in English. In 1967, Mishima published *The Way of the Samurai*, his commentary on the *Hagakure* (literally, *In the Shadow of the Leaves*), a handbook authored by the 18th-century samurai Tsunetomo Yamamoto. In 1968, Mishima published *Sun and Steel*, an autobiographical essay about bodybuilding, martial arts, and the relationship of thought and action which also discusses ritual suicide. (In 1968, Mishima also published a play, *My Friend Hitler*, about the Röhm purge of 1934. He was coy about his true feelings toward Hitler. In truth, he was more a Mussolini man.)

MISHIMA THE ACTIVIST

But Mishima did more than write about action. He acted. In 1967, Mishima enlisted in the Japanese Ground Self-Defense Force (GSDF) and underwent basic training. In 1968, Mishima formed the Tatenokai (Shield Society — Mishima was pleased that the English initials were SS), a private militia composed primarily of Right-wing university students who studied martial arts and swore to protect Japanese tradition against the forces of modernization, Left or Right.

In 1968 and 1969, when Leftist student agitators had the universities in chaos, Mishima participated in debates and teach-ins, criticizing Marxism and arguing that Japanese nationalism, symbolized by loyalty to the Emperor, should come before all other political commitments.

On November 25, 1970, after a year of planning, Mishima and four members of the Shield Society visited the Icigaya Barracks of the Japanese Self-Defense force and took the commander hostage. Mishima demanded that the troops be assembled so he could address them. He had alerted the press in advance. He stepped out onto a balcony in his uniform to harangue the assembled troops, calling them to reject American-imposed materialism and to return to the role of guardians of Japanese tradition.

The speech was largely drowned out by circling helicopters, and the soldiers jeered. Mishima returned to the commander's office, where he and one of his followers, Masakatsu Morita, committed *seppuku*, a ritual suicide involving self-disembowelment with a dagger followed by decapitation with a sword wielded by one's second.

Mishima's stunt is often referred to as a "coup attempt," but this is stupid. Mishima had been talking about, writing about, rehearsing, and preparing for suicide for years. He had no intention of surviving, much less taking power. His death was an attempt to inspire a revival of samurai tradition. In samurai fashion, he wanted a death that mattered, a death of his choosing, a death that he staged with consummate dramatic skill.

Mishima also wished to avoid the decay of old age. Having come to physical health so late in life, he had no intention of experiencing its progressive loss. (His last novel, *The Decay of the Angel*, paints a very bleak portrait of old age.)

Schrader's depiction of Mishima's suicide is far less graphic than *Patriotism* but every bit as powerful. He saves the climaxes of *The Temple of the Golden Pavilion*, *Kyoko's House*, and *Runaway Horses* to the very end, inter-cutting them with Mishima's own suicide, to shattering effect.

This is a great movie, which will leave a lasting impression.

Mishima's Legacy

In the end, though, what did Mishima's death mean? What did it matter? What did it accomplish?

It would be all too easy to dismiss Mishima as a neurotic and a narcissist who engaged in politics as a kind of therapy. Right-wing politics is crawling with such people (none of them with Mishima's talents, unfortunately), and we would be better off without them. If a white equivalent of Mishima wished to write for Counter-Currents/*North American New Right*, we would welcome his work (as we would welcome translations of Mishima's works!). But we would also keep him at arm's length. Such people should be locked in a room with a computer and fed through a slot in the door. They should not be put in positions of trust and responsibility.

But Mishima is safely dead, and the meaning of his death cannot be measured in terms of crass political "deliverables." Indeed, it is a repudiation of the whole calculus of interests that lies at the foundation of modern politics.

Modern politics is based on the idea that a long and comfortable life is the highest value, to be purchased even at the price of our dignity. Aristocratic politics is based on the idea that honor is the highest value, to be purchased even at the price of our lives.

The spiritual aristocrat, therefore, must be ready to die; he must conquer his fear of death; he even must come to love death, for his ability to choose death before dishonor is what raises him above being a mere clever animal. It is what makes him a free man, a natural master rather than a natural slave. It is ultimately the foundation of all forms of higher culture, which involve the rejection or subordination and stylization of merely animal desire.

A natural slave is someone who is willing to give up his honor to save his life. Thus modern politics, which exalts the long and prosperous life as the highest value, is a form of spiritual slavery, even if the external controls are merely soft commercial and political incentives rather than chains and cages.

Thus Mishima's eroticization of death is not a mental illness needing medication. By ceasing to fear death, Mishima became free to lead his life, to take risks other men would not have taken. By ceasing to fear death, Mishima could preserve his honor from the compromises of commerce and politics and the ravages of old age. By ceasing to fear death, Mishima entered into the realm of freedom that is the basis of all high culture. By ceasing to fear death, Mishima struck a mortal blow at the foundations of the modern world.

In my review of Christopher Nolan's *The Dark Knight*, I argued that the Joker is Hollywood's image of a man who is totally free from modern society because he has fundamentally rejected its ruling values—by overcoming the fear of death. An army of such men could bring down the modern world.

Well, Yukio Mishima was a real example of such a man. And, as usual, the truth is stranger than fiction.

Afterword

In my reviews of Christopher Nolan's *Batman Begins* and Guillermo del Toro's *Hellboy* and *Hellboy II: The Golden Army*, I argued that somebody in Hollywood and the comic book/graphic novel industry must be reading up on Traditionalism, for the supervillains in these movies can be seen as Traditionalists. Since Traditionalism is the most fundamental rejection of the modern world, weaponized Traditionalists make the most dramatically potent foils for liberal, democratic, humanistic superheroes like Hellboy and Batman.

Well, shortly after I wrote that, Savitri Devi's *Impeachment of Man* was ordered by someone at one of the major comics companies.

I can see it all now. Somewhere down the line, Hellboy will be squaring off against the Cat Lady of Calcutta, who rises from the Antarctic ice with her fleet of Zündelsaucers, and Batman will face his new arch-nemesis . . . a five-foot samurai with spindly legs in tights.

Counter-Currents/ North American New Right,
January 21, 2011

The Baader-Meinhof Complex

German director Uli Edel's *The Baader-Meinhof Complex* (2008) is a riveting portrayal of the career of the Red Army Fraction (*Rote Armee Fraktion*), a Left-wing terrorist group better known as the Baader-Meinhof Gang after Andreas Baader and Ulrike Meinhof, two of the group's founders. The other founders were Gudrun Ensslin and Horst Mahler (now a comrade on the Right and a prisoner of conscience in Occupied Germany).

The movie begins in 1967 with student protests of a visit by the Shah of Iran. On June 2, 1967, Benno Ohnesorg, one of the protestors, was shot in the head and killed by a police officer, Karl-Heinz Kurras. After the fall of East Germany, it was revealed that Kurras was an agent of the East German secret police, the Stasi. Apparently, he killed Ohnesorg to manufacture a martyr and further radicalize West German students. He succeeded wildly and must be reckoned the godfather of the Baader-Meinhof Gang. (The Stasi later gave direct aid to the RAF.)

Another polarizing event came on April 11, 1968, when student leader Rudi Dutschke was shot three times in the head by a Right-wing assassin Josef Bachmann. (Amazingly, Dutschke survived until 1979, before drowning in a bathtub from a seizure brought on by his wounds.)

Andreas Baader and Gudrun Ensslin began their career as terrorists on April 2, 1968, by setting fire to a department store in protest against the Vietnam War. They were arrested and convicted but fled before sentencing to Rome. Returning to Germany with forged papers, Baader was arrested for reckless driving in a stolen car. Ulrike Meinhof helped him escape custody, during which the group spilled its first blood.

They fled to Jordan to receive training from the PLO but were expelled because of Baader's bad attitude and rejection of military discipline.

Returning to Germany, they pulled off a series of bank robberies, bombings, kidnappings, and assassinations until Baader, Meinhof, and Ensslin, plus Holger Meins and Jan-Carl Raspe, were hunted down and arrested in 1972. (Mahler had been arrested in 1970.)

After the arrest of the leaders, the remaining members launched a new series of bombings, killings, and abductions, plus the seizure of the West German Embassy in Stockholm and the hijacking of a Lufthansa plane. While the first phase of the RAF's violence was directed against American military personnel and Germans who supported NATO and the Vietnam War, the later phase of activity focused entirely on extorting the release of the RAF leaders. (A "third generation" of the RAF operated in the 1980s and '90s until the group announced that it had disbanded in 1998.)

All told, the RAF was responsible for 34 murders, plus robberies, arsons, and bombings that caused countless injuries. In the end, they accomplished absolutely nothing but destruction.

While in prison, the RAF leaders staged several hunger strikes, and Holger Meins died as a result of one on November 9, 1974. On May 21, 1975, Baader, Meinhof, Ensslin, and Raspe went on trial. On May 9, 1976, Ulrike Meinhof was found dead in her cell, hanged with a rope made of strips of towel. Naturally, the surviving members of the group claimed she had been murdered. On April 8, 1977, Baader, Ensslin, and Raspe were convicted of terrorism and multiple murders and attempted murders. They were sentenced to life imprisonment.

After their conviction, the remaining members of the RAF stepped up their campaign of murders and kidnappings, culminating in the hijacking of a Lufthansa plane in Spain by four Arab collaborators on October 13, 1977. They demanded the release of Baader, Ensslin, Raspe, and others. On October 16, they murdered the pilot. On October 18, the plane was assaulted in Mogadishu by an elite German federal police unit. All four hijackers were shot, three of them dying on the spot, and no passengers were seriously injured.

The RAF prisoners heard the announcement of the end of the hijacking on their radios. The next morning, Baader and Raspe were found in their cells, both shot in the head. Baader was dead, and Raspe died in hospital. Ensslin was found hanged. A fourth RAF member, Irmgard Möller, had four stab wounds in her chest but survived. The deaths were ruled a suicide pact, but Möller claimed they had been murdered. (Of course she would.) The movie ends there.

The Baader-Meinhof Complex is an excellent movie, and I recommend it highly. I liked the script, cast, acting, consummate craftsmanship, and captivating storytelling. It has an air of objectivity, and it is hard to say what the director's agenda is. I found the Baader-Meinhof Gang repulsive, but that was probably more a matter of my outlook than the director's. (Actually, I went into this movie *wanting* to like them.) Still, if the director wanted to make pro-Baader-Meinhof propaganda, he would have made a very different movie.

I did not find the Baader-Meinhof Gang repulsive because they were terrorists. After all, they killed and maimed fewer people in 28 years of terrorism than the putative "good guys" killed in 28 seconds at Dresden, Hamburg, Tokyo, Hiroshima, Nagasaki, Baghdad, and the list will only get longer. And although they killed the occasional bystander and other innocents, they were far less ruthless and indiscriminate than the people who use firebombs, nukes, and napalm. How anyone can think that terrorism is worse than war is utterly beyond me.

No, what made the Baader-Meinhof Gang repulsive were their aims and the sick psychology that meshed with them. (From what I have been able to gather online, the movie's portrayal of the personalities, actions, and motivations of the gang members is accurate.)

1. The Baader-Meinhof Gang were paradigmatic deracinated white ethnomasochists and xenophiles. They fought for the Vietnamese and the Palestinians against people of their own blood. If some of them were Jews, one could at least impute a healthy if dissimulated ethnocentrism. But they were all apparently Germans who sincerely hated their own kind. The most shocking expression of this psychology is the fact is that Ulrike Meinhof and Gudrun Ensslin both abandoned their own children in order to devote themselves to revolution.

2. Unsurprisingly, given their hatred of their own kind, Andreas Baader and Gudrun Ensslin are portrayed as spoiled children. The personalities of the rest of the group are less clearly

limned, but we can at least say that they were compatible with Baader and Ensslin for however long they associated with them.

Baader had all the marks of a narcissistic borderline personality: vain, mercurial, manipulative, posturing, chameleon-like, irritable, needy, irrational, arrogant, and, in the end, destructive of all who followed him. The majority of the group consisted of the sort of women—most of them quite attractive—who apparently found such infantile narcissism irresistible. (Perhaps Meinhof and Ensslin abandoned their children because they knew that Baader could suffer the presence of no other infant than himself.)

3. The Baader-Meinhof Gang was less a disciplined revolutionary army than a bunch of hooligans. Getting drunk, stealing sports cars, and firing pistols on midnight joyrides did not advance the group's putative agenda but imperiled it.

The scene at the PLO training camp is priceless: Baader throws a tantrum because he does not like military training and discipline. In a Muslim country, he insists on sharing quarters with his harem who sunbathe with him in the nude. (Yet Ulrike Meinhof was willing to abandon her two daughters to be raised in the Muslim world. Fortunately, their father kidnapped them before this could happen.)

After the leaders were arrested, the remaining gang members focused all their attention on getting them out of jail, not on advancing their larger revolutionary objectives. If Baader *et al.* had been disinterested idealists, they would have directed their followers to abandon them and focus instead on the cause.

4. In the end, Baader, Meinhof, Ensslin, and Raspe were weaklings who preferred suicide to imprisonment. After first confining them in veritable dungeons, the indulgent older generation gave in to the whining of their spoiled children and created a special prison for them, a virtual palace with spacious cells, bookcases, televisions, and radios. (No beanbag chairs or lava lamps were visible in these revolutionary rec rooms.) They were isolated from the tiresome and dangerous company of common criminals and allowed to socialize and collaborate with one another.

Although it seems hard to believe that Baader and Raspe

could have shot themselves in prison, once you see the leniency of the system towards them, one wonders why they even had to *smuggle* guns in. (It is harder to explain how Baader was shot in the *back* of the head, NKVD style, but maybe he was just being a good Communist.)

They had five years (Meinhof dropped out after four) to type out their manifestos and communiqués, grandstand before judges and journalists, direct their followers on the outside with coded messages, etc. They could have carried on the revolution for the rest of their lives, but in the end, emotional self-indulgence meant more to them than their cause, and when they finally gave up on regaining their freedom, they killed themselves.

* * *

The only truthful utterance by any of the terrorists in the whole film comes after the killing of a banker Jürgen Ponto on July 30, 1977, in a botched kidnapping. One of the terrorists wonders why the warmongers of the world are so surprised when they are confronted by blowback in their own homes. It is even more remarkable that more blowback does not occur.

My favorite character in *The Baader-Meinhof Complex* is Horst Herold, played by Bruno Ganz (Hitler in *Downfall*). Herold, born in 1923, is a real-life figure. From 1971 to 1981, he was president of the Bundeskriminalamt (Federal Criminal Department), an arm of the West German state security apparatus tasked with bringing down the RAF.

Herold is portrayed as a model of disinterested idealism, methodical rationality, and Aryan dutifulness. His remarks on terrorism bring to mind Carl Schmitt. He is the perfect foil to Baader and company. The West German government was lucky to have people like him on its side. If Herold's virtues were wedded to the methods of the Baader-Meinhof Gang, the system's days would be numbered.

Counter-Currents/*North American New Right*,
August 27, 2010

ABOUT THE AUTHOR

TREVOR LYNCH is a pen name of Greg Johnson, Ph.D., Editor-in-Chief of Counter-Currents Publishing Ltd. and Editor of its webzine, http://www.counter-currents.com/, and annual journal *North American New Right*. From 2007 to 2010 he was Editor of *The Occidental Quarterly*. In 2009, he created *TOQ Online* with Michael J. Polignano and was its Editor for its first year.

He is the author of *Confessions of a Reluctant Hater* (San Francisco: Counter-Currents, 2010) and *New Right vs. Old Right* (San Francisco: Counter-Currents, 2013).

He is editor of Alain de Benoist, *On Being a Pagan*, trans. Jon Graham (Atlanta: Ultra, 2004); Michael O'Meara, *Toward the White Republic* (San Francisco: Counter-Currents, 2010); Michael J. Polignano, *Taking Our Own Side* (San Francisco: Counter-Currents, 2010); Collin Cleary, *Summoning the Gods: Essays on Paganism in a God-Forsaken World* (San Francisco: Counter-Currents, 2011); Irmin Vinson, *Some Thoughts on Hitler & Other Essays* (San Francisco: Counter-Currents, 2011); *North American New Right*, volume 1 (San Francisco: Counter-Currents, 2012); Kerry Bolton, *Artists of the Right: Resisting Decadence* (San Francisco: Counter-Currents, 2012); James J. O'Meara, *The Homo & the Negro: Masculinist Meditations on Politics & Popular Culture* (San Francisco: Counter-Currents, 2012), and Jonathan Bowden, *Pulp Fascism: Reactionary Themes in Comics, Graphic Novels, & Popular Literature* (San Francisco: Counter-Currents, 2013).

www.ingramcontent.com/pod-product-compliance
Lightning Source LLC
Chambersburg PA
CBHW031628160426
43196CB00006B/320